x⁷5 $ 2⁵0

AN ESSAY OF DRAMATIC POESY
AND OTHER CRITICAL WRITINGS

The Library of Liberal Arts

OSKAR PIEST, FOUNDER

E. Robertson

An Essay of Dramatic Poesy

A Defence of an Essay of Dramatic Poesy

Preface to the Fables

JOHN DRYDEN

Edited, with an Introduction and Notes, by

John L. Mahoney

The Library of Liberal Arts
published by
THE BOBBS-MERRILL COMPANY, INC.
INDIANAPOLIS · NEW YORK

John Dryden: 1631–1700

COPYRIGHT © 1965
THE BOBBS-MERRILL COMPANY, INC.
Printed in the United States of America
Library of Congress Catalog Card Number 65-26522
ISBN-0-672-60298-9 (pbk)
Third Printing

Preface

THIS EDITION of major critical essays of John Dryden provides for students of literature and for the general reading public a collection that embodies some of the many facets of Dryden's complex critical viewpoint. It is my hope that this volume, with complete texts of the great critic's major essays on literary theory, will offer readers the several contributions that mark him as a judge of literature.

Although the responsibility for whatever shortcomings this book may have is mine, I must express my deepest thanks to those who aided in its preparation. My colleagues in the Department of English at Boston College, particularly Professors P. Albert Duhamel, Edward Hirsh, Richard Hughes, John McAleer, Maurice Quinlan, and Donald Sands, have helped me in ways too numerous to mention. Professor Joseph Figurito of the Department of Modern Languages, Boston College, was most kind in assisting me with the translation from the Italian.

I would also like to express my thanks to Mrs. Margaret Hawes and Miss Kathleen Stein for their assistance in the preparation of the manuscript and to Boston College for a faculty grant that was of considerable help.

CONTENTS

Introduction

JOHN DRYDEN's versatility as a man of letters is indisputable; he figures prominently in literary history as a poet, satirist, dramatist, translator, and critic. Of all these varied literary activities his work as a critic is among the most significant. For T. S. Eliot he was "positively the first master of English criticism." [1] Indeed it is Dryden the critical pioneer who quickly captures the imagination of the student of his work. His contributions to genre criticism, to contemporary conceptions of nature and art, and to the social and comparative dimensions of criticism command attention. Although he lived and moved in the great tradition of neoclassicism, he represents a position that is more liberal, more humane, and more searching than those of the Renaissance and early seventeenth century.

It is almost impossible to study Dryden as a critic apart from the religious, philosophical, political, and social phenomena of the age in which he lived. An era that was marked by the incessant warfare between Anglican and Puritan, the ascendancy of Cartesian-Hobbesian rationalism, the dramatic development of science, the overturning of the monarchy of Charles I, the civil warfare from 1642–1660, the Restoration, and the Glorious Revolution of 1688, certainly had a significant effect on the sensibility of the artist. Perhaps such an age, with its shifting allegiances, doubts, and insecurities, might explain to some extent the many so-called inconsistencies in Dryden's career—his shift from Puritan to Anglican to Roman Catholic in religion, from republican to royalist in politics, from one point of view to another in literary criticism.

Even more fundamental to a consideration of the man and his age are the pronounced skeptical tendency of Dryden's

[1] *John Dryden: The Poet, the Dramatist, the Critic* (New York: Terence and Elsa Holliday, 1932), p. 51.

nature, brilliantly sketched by Professor Bredvold in *The Intellectual Milieu of John Dryden,* and his lifelong zest and love for literature. These elements account in large part for his desire to test rules and doctrines, to be skeptical of authority for its own sake, to be always mindful of current taste—in short, to be flexible and open-minded in the craft of the critic. Hence, against the background of rigid neoclassic theory, he must always be seen as part of a liberal element defending the tradition, but always searching for ways of broadening it to include whatever is genuinely artistic; insisting on the importance of delight and entertainment; defending the values of decorum, form, and reasonableness, but leaving room for delights of imagination and emotion.

W. P. Ker has said that Dryden's critical essays "belong to the history of the Renaissance" in that they are part of a critical tradition that attempts to come to an understanding of "the ideals of literature which had been imposed upon it by the learning of classical scholars." [2] To appreciate Dryden's critical freedom, one must measure his statements against the tradition of authority in which he wrote, the tradition of Jonson and Rymer, against the many discussions of the abstract ideas of epic and drama by men like Hobbes, Davenant, and Milton. For Dryden, the rules are undoubtedly important as a great heritage of wisdom, or, as Professor Bate has suggested, as a means of imitating "an ordered, harmonious nature," as aids to the artist in presenting, "as in nature itself," a well-organized and probable action in which each part "contributes to the central design." [3] Inspiration is always the beginning of art. "For my part," says Dryden in *An Essay of Heroic Plays,* "I am of opinion, that neither Homer, Virgil, Statius, Ariosto, Tasso, nor our English Spencer, could have formed their poems half so beautiful, without those gods and

[2] *Essays of John Dryden* (Oxford: Clarendon Press, 1900), I, xv. Hereafter cited as Ker.

[3] Walter Jackson Bate, *Criticism: The Major Texts* (New York: Harcourt, Brace and Company, 1952), p. 126.

spirits, and those enthusiastic parts of poetry, which compose the most noble parts of all their writings." [4]

In the great debate on the relative literary excellence of the ancients and the moderns, Dryden, solidly on the side of the moderns, did much to strengthen and clarify such central ideas in literary theory as nature and art, imitation, the genres, and decorum, as well as the nature, meaning, and value of previous works. In dealing with nature, he stresses its variety and complexity in opposition to the static regularity advanced by earlier theorists. To him nature is not an abstract standard of excellence or a stereotype but "a thing so almost infinite and boundless, as can never fully be comprehended, but where the images of all things are always present." [5] His great watchword is "Whatever is, or may be, is not properly unnatural." [6] Consequently the artist must capture some of the abundance of this nature, its unity and diversity, its joy and sorrow; must, in the fashion of Chaucer and Shakespeare, give us God's plenty, must see the truth vividly and imaginatively. Art then becomes less a process of photography, more a process of imitation, of mimesis in the Aristotelian sense. |

Dryden, in spite of his strong emphasis on common sense, order, and rational control, nevertheless did succeed in freeing imagination from its role as an image-making faculty that it had occupied in too much seventeenth-century criticism and in arguing the case for the imagination's creative potentialities and the freedom of the artist. On the question of the responsibility of the epic poet, he contends that such a poet "is not tied to a bare representation of what is true, or exceeding probable; but that he may let himself loose to visionary objects, and to the representation of such things as depending not on sense, and therefore not to be comprehended by knowledge, may give him a freer scope for imagination." [7] Opposing

---

4 Ker, I, 152–153.
5 *Ibid.*, I, 3.
6 *Ibid.*, I, 154.
7 *Ibid.*, I, 153.

the narrow concept of realism, he clarifies in a vitally new way the concept of mimesis in a manner more truly reminiscent of Aristotle than of many Renaissance codifiers.

For the stage being the representation of the world, and the actions in it, how can it be imagined, that the picture of human life can be more exact than life itself is? He may be allowed sometimes to err, who undertakes to move so many characters and humours, as are requisite in a play, in those narrow channels that are proper to each of them; to conduct his imaginary persons through so many various intrigues and chances, as the labouring audience shall think them lost under every billow; and then at length to work them so naturally out of their distresses, that when the whole plot is laid open, the spectators may rest satisfied that every cause was powerful enough to produce the effect it had; and that the whole chain of them was with such due order linked together, that the first accident would naturally beget the second, till they all rendered the conclusion necessary.[8]

Since for Dryden "to affect the soul, and excite the passions, and, above all, to move admiration (which is the delight of serious plays) . . . is the chief . . . end of poesy, . . . a bare imitation will not serve." [9]

Dryden's general approach to criticism is largely in terms of the genres, or kinds, and the goals and techniques specifically related to each. He writes much about the drama: his general *Essay of Dramatic Poesy*, his *Essay of Heroic Plays*, his *Essay on the Dramatic Poetry of the Last Age*, and his specific discussion of tragedy in the Preface to *Troilus and Cressida*. He deals at length with satire in his *Discourse Concerning the Original and Progress of Satire*, establishing the special function of the genre, which is like moral philosophy in its concern with instruction. His approach to the epic, or heroic poem is seen in works like the Preface to *Annus Mirabilis* and the Dedication of his translation of the *Aeneid*. In defense of his method and specifically in answer to Sir Robert Howard, he contends in the *Defence of An Essay of Dramatic Poesy:* "If he means that there is no essential difference betwixt Comedy, Tragedy, and Farce, but what is only made by the

8 *Ibid.,* I, 2.
9 See below, p. 76.

people's taste, which distinguishes one of them from the other, that is so manifest an error, that I need not lose time to contradict it. Were there neither judge, taste, nor opinion in the world, yet they would differ in their natures; for the action, character, and language of Tragedy, would still be great and high; that of Comedy, lower and more familiar; admiration would be the delight of one, and satire of the other." [10]

Dryden also sets the pace in sociological criticism. Solidly aware of the claims of tradition, he nevertheless feels that the "genius of every age is different" [11] and that the critic must be in touch with the spirit of the age in which a work of art is produced. Dryden exemplifies other critical approaches also. His discussion of French and English drama is a fine example of comparative criticism. His remarks on Elizabethan drama, on Chaucer, and on a variety of other subjects make him one of the first eulogistic or appreciative critics.

He makes great and long-range contributions to English criticism in his treatment of the nature and meaning of previous works of art. His approach to Shakespeare sets the method for the best Shakespearean criticism for the next hundred years. His judgment that Chaucer's "Knight's Tale" is "not much inferior to the *Ilias,* or the *Aeneis*" [12] opens up the possibilities of studying the meaning and mode of the tale in terms of epic theory and technique. In almost every area Dryden is notable for the freshness and distinctiveness of his approach. The extent of his success can be more fully appreciated by a consideration of specific critical works; only in these can the practical applications of the principles and ideas discussed above be seen in a comprehensive way.

The most famous of Dryden's critical endeavors is *An Essay of Dramatic Poesy* (1668). On June 3, 1665, as four courtly gentlemen sail leisurely down the Thames, a literary discussion concerning contemporary poetry develops, in which two fundamental oppositions emerge, one between the classic and

10 Page 81.
11 Page 65.
12 Page 115.

the modern, the other between the Elizabethan and the modern. The first three speakers represent three distinct brands of classicism. Crites is the extremist, arguing that the ancients had fully discovered and embodied those rules to which the moderns should conform. Eugenius, unwilling blindly to revere that which is old simply because it is old, takes the viewpoint that the ancient poets failed to carry out the rules set down by their critics and that, as a matter of fact, the work of the modern writers best illustrates these rules. Lisideius, taking still another approach, praises French neoclassic drama for its exemplification of the classic ideal.

Neander, generally regarded as Dryden's spokesman, soon dominates the essay as he recalls Lisideius' earlier definition of a play as "a just and lively image of human nature," and deplores the fact that too much of the discussion has neglected the implications of the word "lively" in its excessive concern with the word "just." The French dramas do have regularity, he agrees, but it is only a static, mechanical regularity. " 'Tis true," he argues, "those beauties of the French poesy are such as will raise perfection higher where it is, but are not sufficient to give it where it is not: they are indeed the beauties of a statue, but not of a man, because not animated with the soul of Poesy, which is imitation of humour and passions." [13] The English drama, particularly tragicomedy, has more passion, more variety; indeed, more truth and a higher unity. This higher unity is not superimposed but natural. As Neander suggests, "If then the parts are managed so regularly, that the beauty of the whole be kept entire, and that the variety become not a perplexed and confused mass of accidents, you will find it infinitely pleasing to be led in a labyrinth of design, where you see some of your way before you, yet discern not the end till you arrive at it." [14] Shakespeare is for Neander the great exemplar of all the qualities prized in English drama. Despite Shakespeare's occasional crudeness and irregularity, "there is a more masculine fancy and greater spirit in

13 Page 38.
14 Page 42.

the writing, than there is in any of the French." [15] In a passage typifying Dryden's approach to Shakespeare and his generally liberal neoclassicism, he compares Ben Jonson as the poet of art with Shakespeare as the poet of nature: "If I would compare him with Shakespeare, I must acknowledge him [Jonson] the more correct poet, but Shakespeare the greater wit. Shakespeare was the Homer, or father of our dramatic poets; Jonson was the Virgil, the pattern of elaborate writing; I admire him, but I love Shakespeare." [16]

One of the most significant features of Dryden's essay is the debate between Crites and Neander over the use of rhyme in serious drama, a debate whose implications touch the very foundations of Dryden's conception of art and imitation. Crites finds rhyme unnatural, not as proper as blank verse for the stage. Neander, cautious but flexible in approach, contends that blank verse is no more natural than rhyme, that critics have confused the use and abuse of rhyme, and that art depends on a process of selection and heightening. "A play, as I have said, to be like Nature, is to be set above it; as statues which are placed on high are made greater than the life, that they may descend to the sight in their just proportion." [17]

It is this concern with artistic latitude, with imaginative freedom, that pervades Dryden's *Defence of an Essay of Dramatic Poesy,* another excellent example of the flexibility of the critic's mind and the wonderful good sense he brings to his examination of literature. Written as an answer to Sir Robert Howard's objection to the defense of rhyme in the original essay, it is a sparkling examination and defense of the foundations of literature. In dealing with Howard's arguments, he demonstrates the bent for ratiocination which is such a distinctive feature of his work. Finding the debate over rhyme a futile one, he argues that it is not the aim of art to copy nature, but rather to imitate and heighten it, that "if all the enemies of verse will confess as much, I shall not need to prove

[15] Page 47.
[16] Page 50.
[17] Page 67.

that it is natural. I am satisfied if it cause delight; for delight is the chief, if not the only, end of poesy: instruction can be admitted but in the second place, for poesy only instructs as it delights." [18] Dryden's desire to free criticism from the rigidly moralistic approach of critics like Rymer and Dennis did not exclude a concern for the moral influence of great art. "Moral truth," he insists, "is the mistress of the poet as much as of the philosopher; Poesy must resemble natural truth, but it must *be* ethical. Indeed, the poet dresses truth, and adorns nature, but does not alter them." [19] In opposing Howard's idea that the action of stage plays has no reality, and that plays improbably and flagrantly violate the unities of time and place, he offers a most forceful defense of the truth of imagination and of poetry's imitation of nature. Assigning far greater stature to the imagination than Hobbes's mechanistic psychology did, he sees the faculty as creative, as capable of revealing truth. "Imagination," he says, "in a man, or reasonable creature, is supposed to participate of Reason, and when that governs, as it does in the belief of fiction, Reason is not destroyed, but misled, or blinded; that can prescribe to the Reason, during the time of the representation, somewhat like a weak belief of what it sees and hears; and Reason suffers itself to be so hoodwinked, that it may better enjoy the pleasures of the fiction: but it is never so wholly made a captive, as to be drawn headlong into a persuasion of those things which are most remote from probability." [20]

Dryden's last twenty years were devoted more and more to modernizing, translating, and critical writing. In his criticism one feels at first that he is inaugurating a return to the Jonsonian stress of imitation of ancient models, but the further one proceeds, the more one becomes aware that Dryden is continuing to broaden the whole concept of imitation in a way that anticipates the work of Samuel Johnson and Sir Joshua Reynolds

18 Page 76.
19 Page 83.
20 Page 88.

His memorable Preface to the *Fables* is mellow and retrospective, a drawing together of the many facets of his approach to literature. It is a striking example of his characteristic effort to mediate between the extremes of much rigid contemporary criticism: between tradition and original genius, between the rule of reason and the rule of imagination, between the moral and aesthetic concerns of art. At the same time it reveals his underlying and consistent allegiance to certain neoclassic ideals which he associated with greatness in literature and art.

His concern with the moral, for example, can be seen in his statement that he has written "nothing which savours of immorality or profaneness," and that he has chosen such fables "as contain in each of them some instructive moral," [21] echoing his earlier praise of Shakespeare's *Antony and Cleopatra* in the Preface to *All for Love* (1678) as a story with the moral of unlawful love punished.

His famous discussion of Chaucer, regarded by Caroline Spurgeon as the first detailed and careful criticism of Chaucer and the first comparison of the English poet with Ovid,[22] reveals most clearly the two sides of Dryden as a critic; his fundamental dedication to the neoclassic ideal, but always tempered by his desire to see the ideal in its full range of possibilities, to leave an appeal always open from criticism to nature. Accordingly, his treatment of Chaucer is very much along the lines of his criticism of Shakespeare. Chaucer is a "diamond in the rough," a poet with more nature than wit, with a rough, unpolished genius, a Homer rather than a Virgil.

His merits, however, always outweigh his weaknesses. "Chaucer followed Nature everywhere," [23] capturing its variety and abundance; he possessed a "wonderful comprehensive

---

21 Pages 97–98.

22 Caroline F. E. Spurgeon, *Five Hundred Years of Chaucer Criticism and Allusion (1357–1900)* (London and New York: Oxford University Press, 1914–1925), I, xxxvii.

23 Page 104.

nature." [24] Concluding with a passage that seems to combine so many aspects of his approach to literary criticism, the sociological, the appreciative, and the analytic, Dryden writes:

> He has taken into the compass of his *Canterbury Tales* the various manners and humours (as we now call them) of the whole English nation, in his age. Not a single character has escaped him. All his pilgrims are severally distinguished from each other; and not only in their inclinations, but in their very physiognomies and persons. . . . The matter and manner of their tales, and of their telling, are so suited to their different educations, humours, and callings, that each of them would be improper in any other mouth. Even the grave and serious characters are distinguished by their several sorts of gravity: their discourses are such as belong to their age, their calling, and their breeding; such as are becoming of them and of them only.[25]

Samuel Johnson wrote that "the criticism of Dryden is the criticism of a poet; not a dull collection of theorems, nor a rude detection of faults, which perhaps the censor was not able to have committed; but a gay and vigorous dissertation, where delight is mingled with instruction, and where the author proves his right of judgment, by his power of performance." [26] One feels that Johnson here captures the essential spirit of the man and his work. Always humane and liberal, a believer in progress and modernity, Dryden is a major spokesman for the Augustan ideal of literature. His contributions to English criticism are major ones.

JOHN L. MAHONEY

Chestnut Hill, Massachusetts
July 1965

---

[24] Page 108.
[25] Page 108.
[26] Samuel Johnson, *Selected Prose and Poetry*, ed. Bertrand Bronson (New York: Holt, Rinehart and Winston, 1952), p. 474.

Selected Bibliography

AN EXCELLENT bibliographical guide to Dryden studies is Hugh Macdonald's *John Dryden: A Bibliography of Early Editions and Drydeniana.* Oxford: Clarendon Press, 1939.

Editions of Dryden's Criticism

The Essays of John Dryden, ed. W. P. KER. 2 vols. Oxford: Clarendon Press, 1900.

Of Dramatic Poesy and Other Critical Essays, ed. GEORGE WATSON. 2 vols. London and New York: J. M. Dent and Sons, Ltd., and E. P. Dutton and Co., Inc., 1962.

Collateral Reading

ABRAMS, MEYER. *The Mirror and the Lamp.* New York: Oxford University Press, 1952.

ADEN, JOHN. *Critical Opinions of John Dryden: A Dictionary.* Nashville: Vanderbilt University Press, 1963.

——. "Dryden and Boileau: The Question of Critical Influence," *Studies in Philology,* L (1953), 491–509.

——. "Dryden and the Imagination: The First Phase," PMLA, LXXIV (1959), 28-50.

ATKINS, J. W. H. *English Literary Criticism: Seventeenth and Eighteenth Centuries.* London: Methuen and Co., Ltd., 1951.

BATE, WALTER J. *From Classic to Romantic.* Cambridge, Mass.: Harvard University Press, 1946.

BREDVOLD, LOUIS. *The Intellectual Milieu of John Dryden.* Ann Arbor: University of Michigan Press, 1934.

CRANE, R. S. "English Neoclassical Criticism: An Outline Sketch," in *Critics and Criticism, Ancient and Modern,* ed. R. S. CRANE. Chicago: University of Chicago Press, 1952. Pp. 375–388.

ELIOT, T. S. *John Dryden: The Poet, the Dramatist, the Critic.* New York: Terence and Elsa Holliday, 1932.

HATHAWAY, BAXTER. "John Dryden and the Function of Tragedy," *PMLA,* LVIII (1934), 665–673.

HUNTLEY, FRANK. *On Dryden's Essay of Dramatic Poesy.* Ann Arbor: University of Michigan Contributions in Modern Philology, 1951.

LEGOUIS, PIERRE. "Corneille and Dryden as Dramatic Critics," in *Seventeenth Century Studies Presented to Sir Herbert Grierson.* Oxford: Clarendon Press, 1938. Pp. 269–291.

SAINTSBURY, GEORGE. *John Dryden.* London: Macmillan and Co., 1894.

SHERWOOD, JOHN C. "Dryden and the Rules: *The Preface to the Fables,*" *Journal of English and Germanic Philology,* LII (1953), 13–26.

SMITH, DAVID NICHOL. *John Dryden.* Cambridge, England: Cambridge University Press, 1950.

TROBRIDGE, HOYT. "The Place of Rules in Dryden's Criticism," *Modern Philology,* XLIV (1946), 84–96.

VAN DOREN, MARK. *John Dryden: A Study of His Poetry.* New York: Henry Holt and Company, 1946.

WARD, CHARLES A. *The Life of John Dryden.* Chapel Hill, N.C.: The University of North Carolina Press, 1961.

WILLIAMSON, GEORGE. "The Occasion of *An Essay of Dramatic Poesy,*" *Modern Philology,* XLIV (1946), 1–9.

WIMSATT, W. K., and BROOKS, CLEANTH. *Literary Criticism: A Short History.* New York: Alfred Knopf, 1957.

Note on the Text

THE TEXT used is that of W. P. Ker in *Essays of John Dryden* (Oxford: Clarendon Press, 1900). This text is one that has been carefully collated with the original editions. For the convenience of the reader, the editor has translated foreign language references, identified sources, and provided footnotes. Needless to say, Dryden's Latin leaves much to be desired.

J. L. M.

AN ESSAY OF DRAMATIC POESY
AND OTHER CRITICAL WRITINGS

An Essay of Dramatic Poesy

[1668]

IT WAS that memorable day,[1] in the first summer of the
late war, when our navy engaged the Dutch; a day wherein
the two most mighty and best appointed fleets which any age
had ever seen, disputed the command of the greater half of the
globe, the commerce of nations, and the riches of the universe.
While these vast floating bodies, on either side, moved against
each other in parallel lines, and our countrymen, under the
happy conduct of his Royal Highness, went breaking, by little
and little, into the line of the enemies; the noise of the cannon
from both navies reached our ears about the City, so that all
men being alarmed with it, and in a dreadful suspense of the
event which we knew was then deciding, every one went following the sound as his fancy led him; and leaving the town
almost empty, some took towards the park, some cross the
river, others down it; all seeking the noise in the depth
of silence.

Among the rest, it was the fortune of Eugenius, Crites,
Lisideius, and Neander,[2] to be in company together; three of
them persons whom their wit and quality have made known
to all the town; and whom I have chose to hide under these
borrowed names, that they may not suffer by so ill a relation
as I am going to make of their discourse.

Taking then a barge which a servant of Lisideius had provided for them, they made haste to shoot the bridge, and left

---

[1] June 3, 1665.

[2] Much has been written about the identity of the speakers in the
Essay, but there is now general agreement that Eugenius is Charles Sack-
ville (1638–1706), son of Richard, fifth Earl of Dorset; that Crites is Sir
Robert Howard (1626–1698); that Lisideius is Sir Charles Sedley (*ca.*
1639–1701); and that Neander is Dryden himself.

behind them that great fall of waters which hindered them from hearing what they desired: after which, having disengaged themselves from many vessels which rode at anchor in the Thames, and almost blocked up the passage towards Greenwich, they ordered the watermen to let fall their oars more gently; and then, every one favouring his own curiosity with a strict silence, it was not long ere they perceived the air break about them like the noise of distant thunder, or of swallows in a chimney: those little undulations of sound, though almost vanishing before they reached them, yet still seeming to retain somewhat of their first horror, which they had betwixt the fleets. After they had attentively listened till such time as the sound by little and little went from them, Eugenius, lifting up his head, and taking notice of it, was the first who congratulated to the rest that happy omen of our Nation's victory: adding, we had but this to desire in confirmation of it, that we might hear no more of that noise, which was now leaving the English coast. When the rest had concurred in the same opinion, Crites, a person of a sharp judgment, and somewhat too delicate a taste in wit, which the world have mistaken in him for ill-nature, said, smiling to us, that if the concernment of this battle had not been so exceeding great, he could scarce have wished the victory at the price he knew he must pay for it, in being subject to the reading of so many ill verses as he was sure would be made upon it. Adding, that no argument could scape some of those eternal rhymers, who watch a battle with more diligence than the ravens and birds of prey; and the worst of them surest to be first in upon the quarry: while the better able either out of modesty writ not at all, or set that due value upon their poems, as to let them be often called for and long expected! 'There are some of those impertinent people you speak of,' answered Lisideius, 'who to my knowledge are already so provided, either way, that they can produce not only a Panegyric upon the victory, but, if need be, a Funeral Elegy on the Duke; and after they have crowned his valour with many laurels, at last deplore the odds under which he fell, concluding that his courage deserved a better destiny.' All the company smiled at the conceit of Lisideius; but Crites, more eager than before, began to make particular exceptions against some writers, and said, the public magistrate ought to send betimes to forbid them; and that it concerned the peace and quiet of all honest people, that ill poets should be as well silenced as seditious preachers. 'In my opinion,' replied Eugenius, 'you pursue your point too far; for as to my own particular, I am so great a lover of poesy, that I could wish them all rewarded, who attempt but to do well; at least, I would not have them worse used than Sylla the Dictator did one of their brethren heretofore:—*Quem in concione vidimus* (says Tully) *cum ei libellum malus poëta de populo subjecisset, quod epigramma in eum fecisset tantummodo alternis versibus longiusculis, statim ex iis rebus quas tunc vendebat jubere ei praemium tribui, sub ea conditione ne quid postea scriberet.*'[3] 'I could wish with all my heart,' replied Crites, 'that many whom we know were as bountifully thanked upon the same condition— that they would never trouble us again. For amongst others, I have a mortal apprehension of two poets,[4] whom this victory, with the help of both her wings, will never be able to escape. ' 'Tis easy to guess whom you intend,' said Lisideius; and without naming them, I ask you, if one of them does not perpetually pay us with clenches upon words, and a certain clownish kind of raillery? if now and then he does not offer at a catachresis or Clevelandism,[5] wresting and torturing a word into another meaning: in fine, if he be not one of those whom the French would call *un mauvais buffon;* one that is so much

[3] "Whom we saw in a gathering, when an amateurish poet of the people handed up a book to him with every other line a bit longer; immediately from those wares which he was then selling, he ordered a reward to be given to him but on the condition that he would not write afterwards" (Cicero, *Pro Archia* X. 25).

[4] One of these was probably Robert Wild; the other Richard Flecknoe, satirized by Dryden in "Mac Flecknoe."

[5] John Cleveland (1613–1658), an extreme representative of metaphysical poetry, whose style is characterized by puns, farfetched conceits, etc.

a well-willer to the satire, that he spares no man; and though
he cannot strike a blow to hurt any, yet ought to be punished
for the malice of the action, as our witches are justly hanged,
because they think themselves so; and suffer deservedly for
believing they did mischief, because they meant it.' 'You have
described him,' said Crites, 'so exactly, that I am afraid to
come after you with my other extremity of poetry. He is one
of those who, having had some advantage of education and
converse, knows better than the other what a poet should be,
but puts it into practice more unluckily than any man; his
style and matter are everywhere alike: he is the most calm,
peaceable writer you ever read: he never disquiets your passions with the least concernment, but still leaves you in as even
a temper as he found you; he is a very Leveller in poetry: he
creeps along with ten little words in every line, and helps out
his numbers with *For to,* and *Unto,* and all the pretty exple-
tives he can find, till he drags them to the end of another
line; while the sense is left tired half way behind it: he doubly
starves all his verses, first for want of thought, and then of
expression; his poetry neither has wit in it, nor seems to have
it; like him in Martial:

> *Pauper videri* Cinna *vult, est pauper.*[6]

'He affects plainness, to cover his want of imagination: when
he writes the serious way, the highest flight of his fancy is some
miserable antithesis, or seeming contradiction; and in the
comic he is still reaching at some thin conceit, the ghost of a
jest, and that too flies before him, never to be caught; these
swallows which we see before us on the Thames are the just
resemblance of his wit: you may observe how near the water
they stoop, how many proffers they make to dip, and yet how
seldom they touch it; and when they do, 'tis but the surface:
they skim over it but to catch a gnat, and then mount into
the air and leave it.'

'Well, gentlemen,' said Eugenius, 'you may speak your
pleasure of these authors; but though I and some few more

---

[6] "Cinna wishes to appear a pauper, and he is" (*Epigrams* VIII. 19).

about the town may give you a peaceable hearing, yet assure yourselves, there are multitudes who would think you malicious and them injured: especially him who you first described; he is the very Withers of the city: they have bought more editions of his works than would serve to lay under all their pies at the Lord Mayor's Christmas. When his famous poem first came out in the year 1660, I have seen them reading it in the midst of 'Change time; nay so vehement they were at it, that they lost their bargain by the candles' ends; but what will you say, if he has been received amongst the great ones? I can assure you he is, this day, the envy of a great Person who is lord in the art of quibbling; and who does not take it well, that any man should intrude so far into his province.' 'All I would wish,' replied Crites, 'is that they who love his writings, may still admire him, and his fellow poet: *Qui Bavium non odit, &c.*,[7] is curse sufficient.' 'And farther,' added Lisideius, 'I believe there is no man who writes well, but would think himself very hardly dealt with, if their admirers should praise anything of his: *Nam quos contemnimus, eorum quoque laudes contemnimus.*'[8] There are so few who write well in this age,' says Crites, 'that methinks any praises should be welcome; they neither rise to the dignity of the last age, nor to any of the Ancients: and we may cry out of the writers of this time, with more reason than Petronius of his, *Pace vestra liceat dixisse, primi omnium eloquentiam perdidists:*[9] you have debauched the true old poetry so far, that Nature, which is the soul of it, is not in any of your writings.'

'If your quarrel,' said Eugenius, 'to those who now write, be grounded only on your reverence to antiquity, there is no man more ready to adore those great Greeks and Romans than I am: but on the other side, I cannot think so contemptibly of the age I live in, or so dishonourably of my own country,

[7] "Who does not hate Boevius, etc." (Virgil, *Eclogues* III. 90).

[8] "For we detest those people who admire what we despise" (source unidentified).

[9] "If I may say it, you [rhetoricians] are the first to have lost the eloquence of all who went before" (*Satyricon* 2).

as not to judge we equal the Ancients in most kinds of poesy, and in some surpass them; neither know I any reason why I may not be as zealous for the reputation of our age, as we find the Ancients themselves in reference to those who lived before them. For you hear your Horace saying,

> *Indignor quidquam reprehendi, non quia crasse*
> *Compositum, illepideve putetur, sed quia nuper.*

And after:

> *Si meliora dies, ut vina, poemata reddit,*
> *Scire velim, pretium chartis quotus arroget annus?*[10]

'But I see I am engaging in a wide dispute, where the arguments are not like to reach close on either side; for Poesy is of so large an extent, and so many both of the Ancients and Moderns have done well in all kinds of it, that in citing one against the other, we shall take up more time this evening than each man's occasions will allow him: therefore I would ask Crites to what part of Poesy he would confine his arguments, and whether he would defend the general cause of the Ancients against the Moderns, or oppose any age of the Moderns against this of ours?'

Crites, a little while considering upon this demand, told Eugenius he approved his propositions, and if he pleased, he would limit their dispute to Dramatic Poesy; in which he thought it not difficult to prove, either that the Ancients were superior to the Moderns, or the last age to this of ours.

Eugenius was somewhat surprised, when he heard Crites make choice of that subject. 'For ought I see,' said he, 'I have undertaken a harder province than I imagined; for though I never judged the plays of the Greek or Roman poets comparable to ours, yet, on the other side, those we now see acted come short of many which were written in the last age: but my comfort is, if we are o'ercome, it will be only by our own coun-

[10] "I am disturbed that something is blamed not because it is poorly constructed and dull, but because it is new" (*Epistles* II. 1. 76–77); and "If age makes poems superior as it does wines, I would like to know how many years are required for the process" (*ibid.*, 34–35).

trymen: and if we yield to them in this one part of poesy, we more surpass them in all the other: for in the epic or lyric way, it will be hard for them to show us one such amongst them, as we have many now living, or who lately were so: they can produce nothing so courtly writ or which expresses so much the conversation of a gentleman, as Sir John Suckling; nothing so even, sweet, and flowing, as Mr. Waller; nothing so majestic, so correct, as Sir John Denham; nothing so elevated, so copious, and full of spirit, as Mr. Cowley; [11] as for the Italian, French, and Spanish plays, I can make it evident, that those who now write surpass them; and that the Drama is wholly ours.'

All of them were thus far of Eugenius his opinion, that the sweetness of English verse was never understood or practised by our fathers; even Crites himself did not much oppose it: and every one was willing to acknowledge how much our poesy is improved by the happiness of some writers yet living; who first taught us to mould our thoughts into easy and significant words; to retrench the superfluities of expression, and to make our rime so properly a part of the verse, that it should never mislead the sense, but itself be led and governed by it.

Eugenius was going to continue this discourse, when Lisideius told him it was necessary, before they proceeded further, to take a standing measure of their controversy; for how was it possible to be decided who writ the best plays, before we know what a play should be? But, this once agreed on by both parties, each might have recourse to it, either to prove his own advantages, or to discover the failings of his adversary.

He had no sooner said this, but all desired the favour of him to give the definition of a play; and they were the more importunate, because neither Aristotle, nor Horace, nor any other, who write of that subject, had ever done it.

Lisideius, after some modest denials, at last confessed he had a rude notion of it; indeed, rather a description than a definition; but which served to guide him in his private thoughts,

[11] Sir John Suckling (1609–1642), Edmund Waller (1606–1687), Sir John Denham (1615–1669), Abraham Cowley (1618–1667)—all English poets.

when he was to make a judgment of what others writ: that he
conceived a play ought to be, *A just and lively image of
human nature, representing its passions and humours, and
the changes of fortune to which it is subject, for the delight
and instruction of mankind.*

This definition, though Crites raised a logical objection
against it; that it was only *a genere et fine*,[12] and so not altogether perfect; was yet well received by the rest: and after they
had given order to the watermen to turn their barge, and row
softly, that they might take the cool of the evening in their
return, Crites, being desired by the company to begin, spoke
on behalf of the Ancients, in this manner:

'If confidence presage a victory, Eugenius, in his own
opinion, has already triumphed over the Ancients: nothing
seems more easy to him, than to overcome those whom it is
our greatest praise to have imitated well; for we do not only
build upon their foundation, but by their models. Dramatic
Poesy had time enough, reckoning from Thespis (who first
invented it) to Aristophanes, to be born, to grow up, and to
flourish in maturity. It has been observed of arts and sciences,
that in one and the same century they have arrived to a great
perfection; and no wonder, since every age has a kind of universal genius, which inclines those that live in it to some particular studies: the work then being pushed on by many hands,
must of necessity go forward.

'Is it not evident, in these last hundred years (when the
study of philosophy has been the business of all the Virtuosi
in Christendom), that almost a new Nature has been revealed
to us?—that more errors of the school have been detected, more
useful experiments in philosophy have been made, more noble
secrets in optics, medicine, anatomy, astronomy, discovered,
than in all those credulous and doting ages from Aristotle to
us?—so true is it, that nothing spreads more fast than science,
when rightly and generally cultivated.

'Add to this, the more than common emulation that was in

[12] "General and not specific," i.e., the definition would be valid for
other literary forms as well as drama.

those times of writing well; which though it be found in all ages and all persons that pretend to the same reputation, yet Poesy, being then in more esteem than now it is, had greater honours decreed to the professors of it, and consequently the rivalship was more high between them; they had judges ordained to decide their merit, and prizes to reward it; and historians have been diligent to record of Eschylus, Euripides, Sophocles, Lycophron, and the rest of them, both who they were that vanquished in these wars of the theatre, and how often they were crowned: while the Asian kings and Grecian commonwealths scarce afforded them a nobler subject than the unmanly luxuries of a debauched court, or giddy intrigues of a factious city. *Alit aemulatio ingenia* (says [Velleius] Paterculus) *et nunc invidia, nunc admiratio incitationem accendit*: [13] Emulation is the spur of wit; and sometimes envy, sometimes admiration, quickens our endeavours.

'But now, since the rewards of honour are taken away, that virtuous emulation is turned into direct malice; yet so slothful, that it contents itself to condemn and cry down others, without attempting to do better: 'tis a reputation too unprofitable, to take the necessary pains for it; yet, wishing they had it is incitement enough to hinder others from it. And this, in short, Eugenius, is the reason why you have now so few good poets, and so many severe judges. Certainly, to imitate the Ancients well, much labour and long study is required; which pains, I have already shown, our poets would want encouragement to take, if yet they had ability to go through with it. Those Ancients have been faithful imitators and wise observers of that Nature which is so torn and ill represented in our plays; they have handed down to us a perfect resemblance of her; which we, like ill copiers, neglecting to look on, have rendered monstrous, and disfigured. But, that you may know how much you are indebted to those your masters, and be ashamed to have so ill requited them, I must remember you, that all the rules by which we practise the Drama at this

---

[13] *Res gestae divi augusti (Historia romana)* I. 17. 6. Dryden himself translates the line in the following sentence.

day (either such as relate to the justness and symmetry of the plot, or the episodical ornaments, such as descriptions, narrations, and other beauties, which are not essential to the play) were delivered to us from the observations which Aristotle made, of those poets, which either lived before him, or were his contemporaries: we have added nothing of our own, except we have the confidence to say our wit is better; of which none boast in this our age, but such as understand not theirs. Of that book which Aristotle has left us, περὶ τῆς Ποιητικῆς [*Poetics*], Horace his *Art of Poetry* is an excellent comment, and I believe, restores to us that Second Book of his concerning *Comedy*, which is wanting in him.

'Out of these two have been extracted the famous Rules, which the French call *Des Trois Unitez*, or, the Three Unities, which ought to be observed in every regular play; namely, of Time, Place, and Action.

'The Unity of Time they comprehend in twenty-four hours, the compass of a natural day, or as near as it can be contrived; and the reason of it is obvious to every one—that the time of the feigned action, or fable of the play, should be proportioned as near as can be to the duration of that time in which it is represented: since therefore, all plays are acted on the theatre in a space of time much within the compass of twenty-four hours, that play is to be thought the nearest imitation of nature, whose plot or action is confined within that time; and, by the same rule which concludes this general proportion of time, it follows, that all the parts of it are to be equally subdivided; as namely, that one act take not up the supposed time of half a day, which is out of proportion to the rest; since the other four are then to be straitened within the compass of the remaining half: for it is unnatural that one act, which being spoke or written is not longer than the rest, should be supposed longer by the audience; 'tis therefore the poet's duty, to take care that no act should be imagined to exceed the time in which it is represented on the stage; and that the intervals and inequalities of time be supposed to fall out between the acts.

'This rule of time, how well it has been observed by the Ancients, most of their plays will witness; you see them in their tragedies (wherein to follow this rule, is certainly most difficult) from the very beginning of their plays, falling close into that part of the story which they intend for the action or principal object of it, leaving the former part to be delivered by narration: so that they set the audience, as it were, at the post where the race is to be concluded; and, saving them the tedious expectation of seeing the poet set out and ride the beginning of the course, you behold him not till he is in sight of the goal, and just upon you.

'For the second Unity, which is that of Place, the Ancients meant by it, that the scene ought to be continued through the play, in the same place where it was laid in the beginning: for the stage on which it is represented being but one and the same place, it is unnatural to conceive it many; and those far distant from one another. I will not deny but, by the variation of painted scenes, the fancy, which in these cases will contribute to its own deceit, may sometimes imagine it several places, with some appearance of probability; yet it still carries the greater likelihood of truth, if those places be supposed so near each other, as in the same town or city; which may all be comprehended under the larger denomination of one place; for a greater distance will bear no proportion to the shortness of time which is allotted in the acting, to pass from one of them to another; for the observation of this, next to the Ancients, the French are to be most commended. They tie themselves so strictly to the Unity of Place, that you never see in any of their plays, a scene changed in the middle of an act: if the act begins in a garden, a street, or a chamber, 'tis ended in the same place; and that you may know it to be the same, the stage is so supplied with persons, that it is never empty all the time: he that enters the second, has business with him who was on before; and before the second quits the stage, a third appears who has business with him. This Corneille calls *la liaison des scenes,* the continuity or joining of the scenes; and 'tis a good mark of a well-contrived play, when all the persons are known to each other, and every one of them has some affairs with all the rest.

'As for the third Unity, which is that of Action, the Ancients meant no other by it than what the logicians do by their *finis*, the end or scope of any action; that which is the first in intention, and last in execution: now the poet is to aim at one great and complete action, to the carrying on of which all things in his play, even the very obstacles, are to be subservient; and the reason of this is as evident as any of the former.

'For two actions, equally laboured and driven on by the writer, would destroy the unity of the poem; it would be no longer one play, but two: not but that there may be many actions in a play, as Ben Johnson has observed in his *Discoveries;*[14] but they must be all subservient to the great one, which our language happily expresses in the name of *underplots:* such as in Terence's *Eunuch* is the difference and reconcilement of Thais and Phaedria, which is not the chief business of the play, but promotes the marriage of Chaerea and Chremes's sister, principally intended by the poet. There ought to be but one action, says Corneille, that is, one complete action which leaves the mind of the audience in a full repose; but this cannot be brought to pass but by many other imperfect actions, which conduce to it, and hold the audience in a delightful suspence of what will be.

'If by these rules (to omit many other drawn from the precepts and practice of the Ancients) we should judge our modern plays, 'tis probable that few of them would endure the trial: that which should be business of a day, takes up in some of them an age; instead of one action, they are the epitomes of a man's life; and for one spot of ground (which the stage should represent) we are sometimes in more countries than the map can show us.

'But if we will allow the Ancients to have contrived well, we must acknowledge them to have writ better; questionless we are deprived of a great stock of wit in the loss of Menander

14 *Timber: or Discoveries,* a critical work by Jonson, published in 1640.

among the Greek poets, and of Caecilius, Afranius, and Varius, among the Romans; we may guess at Menander's excellency by the plays of Terence, who translated some of his; and yet wanted so much of him, that he was called by C. Caesar the half-Menander; and may judge of Varius, by the testimonies of Horace, Martial, and Velleius Paterculus. 'Tis probable that these, could they be recovered, would decide the controversy; but so long as Aristophanes in the old Comedy, and Plautus in the new are extant, while the tragedies of Euripides, Sophocles, and Seneca, are to be had, I can never see one of those plays which are now written, but it increases my admiration of the Ancients. And yet I must acknowledge farther, that to admire them as we ought, we should understand them better than we do. Doubtless many things appear flat to us, whose wit depended on some custom or story, which never came to our knowledge; or perhaps on some criticism in their language, which being so long dead, and only remaining in their books, 'tis not possible that they should make us know it perfectly. To read Macrobius,[15] explaining the propriety and elegancy of many words in Virgil, which I had before passed over without consideration, as common things, is enough to assure me that I ought to think the same of Terence; and that in the purity of his style (which Tully so much valued that he ever carried his works about him) there is yet left in him great room for admiration, if I knew but where to place it. In the mean time I must desire you to take notice, that the greatest man of the last age (Ben Johnson) was willing to give place to them in all things: he was not only a professed imitator of Horace, but a learned plagiary of all the others; you track him every where in their snow: if Horace, Lucan, Petronius Arbiter, Seneca, and Juvenal, had their own from him, there are few serious thoughts which are new in him: you will pardon me, therefore, if I presume he loved their fashion, when he wore their clothes. But since I have otherwise great veneration for him, and you, Eugenius, prefer

15 Macrobius, a Roman philosopher and grammarian, wrote around A.D. 400.

him above all other poets, I will use no farther argument to
you than his example: I will produce Father Ben to you,
dressed in all the ornaments and colours of the Ancients; you
will need no other guide to our party, if you follow him; and
whether you consider the bad plays of our age, or regard the
good ones of the last, both the best and worst of the modern
poets will equally instruct you to esteem the Ancients.'

Crites had no sooner left speaking, but Eugenius, who had
waited with some impatience for it, thus began:

'I have observed in your speech, that the former part of it is
convincing as to what the Moderns have profited by the rules
of the Ancients; but in the latter you are careful to conceal
how much they have excelled them; we own all the helps we
have from them, and want neither veneration nor gratitude
while we acknowledge that to overcome them we must make
use of the advantages we have received from them: but to
these assistances we have joined our own industry; for, had we
sat down with a dull imitation of them, we might then have
lost somewhat of the old perfection, but never acquired any
that was new. We draw not therefore after their lines, but those
of Nature; and having the life before us, besides the experience of all they knew, it is no wonder if we hit some airs and
features which they have missed. I deny not what you urge
of arts and sciences, that they have flourished in some ages
more than others; but your instance in philosophy makes for
me: for if natural causes be more known now than in the time
of Aristotle, because more studied, it follows that poesy and
other arts may, with the same pains, arrive still nearer to perfection; and, that granted, it will rest for you to prove that
they wrought more perfect images of human life than we;
which seeing in your discourse you have avoided to make
good, it shall now be my task to show you some part of their
defects, and some few excellencies of the Moderns. And I think
there is none among us can imagine I do it enviously, or with
purpose to detract from them; for what interest of fame or
profit can the living lose by the reputation of the dead? On
the other side, it is a great truth which Velleius Paterculus

affrms: *Audita visis libentius laudamus; et praesentia invidia, praeterita admiratione prosequimur; et his nos obrui, illis instrui credimus:* [16] that praise or censure is certainly the most sincere, which unbribed posterity shall give us.

'Be pleased then in the first place to take notice, that the Greek poesy, which Crites has affirmed to have arrived to perfection in the reign of the Old Comedy, was so far from it, that the distinction of it into acts was not known to them; or if it were, it is yet so darkly delivered to us that we cannot make it out.

[margin note: no act distinctions]

'All we know of it is, from the singing of their Chorus; and that too is so uncertain, that in some of their plays we have reason to conjecture they sung more than five times. Aristotle indeed divides the integral parts of a play into four. First, the *Protasis,* or entrance, which gives light only to the characters of the persons, and proceeds very little into any part of the action. Secondly, the *Epitasis,* or working up of the plot; where the play grows warmer, the design or action of it is drawing on, and you see something promising that it will come to pass. Thirdly, the *Catastasis,* or counterturn, which destroys that expectation, imbroils the action in new difficulties, and leaves you far distant from that hope in which it found you; as you may have observed in a violent stream resisted by a narrow passage,—it runs round to an eddy, and carries back the waters with more swiftness than it brought them on. Lastly, the *Catastrophe,* which the Grecians called λύσις, the French *le denouement,* and we the discovery or unravelling of the plot: there you see all things settling again upon their first foundations; and, the obstacles which hindered the design or action of the play once removed, it ends with that resemblance of truth and nature, that the audience are satisfied with the conduct of it. Thus this great man delivered to us the image of a play; and I must confess it is so lively, that from

[16] "We praise what we hear more freely than what we see; we regard the present with envy, the past with admiration; and we believe we are hurt by the first and instructed by the latter" (*Res gestae divi augusti* [*Historia romana*] II. 92. 5).

thence much light has been derived to the forming it more perfectly into acts and scenes: but what poet first limited to five the number of acts, I know not; only we see it so firmly established in the time of Horace, that he gives it for a rule in comedy; *Neu brevior quinto, neu sit productior actu.*[17] So that you see the Grecians cannot be said to have consummated this art; writing rather by entrances, than by acts, and having rather a general indigested notion of a play, than knowing how and where to bestow the particular graces of it.

'But since the Spaniards at this day allow but three acts, which they call *Jornadas,* to a play, and the Italians in many of theirs follow them, when I condemn the Ancients, I declare it is not altogether because they have not five acts to every play, but because they have not confined themselves to one certain number: it is building an house without a model; and when they succeeded in such undertakings, they ought to have sacrificed to Fortune, not to the Muses.

'Next, for the plot, which Aristotle called τὸ μυθος, and often τῶν πραγμάτων σύνθεσις,[18] and from him the Romans *Fabula,* it has already been judiciously observed by a late writer,[19] that in their tragedies it was only some tale derived from Thebes or Troy, or at least something that happened in those two ages; which was worn so threadbare by the pens of all the epic poets, and even by tradition itself of the talkative Greeklings (as Ben Johnson calls them) that before it came upon the stage, it was already known to all the audience: and the people, so soon as ever they heard the name of Oedipus, knew as well as the poet, that he had killed his father by a mistake, and committed incest with his mother, before the play; that they were now to hear of a great plague, an oracle, and the ghost of Laius: so that they sat with a yawning kind of expectation, till he was to come with his eyes pulled out, and speak a hundred or two of verses in a tragic tone, in complaint of his misfortunes. But one Oedipus, Hercules, or Medea, had

---

[17] "Let it be neither more nor less than five acts" (*Art of Poetry* 189).
[18] "Joining of the actions."
[19] Sir Robert Howard.

been tolerable: poor people, they scaped not so good cheap; they had still the *chapon bouillé* [20] set before them till their appetites were cloyed with the same dish, and, the novelty being gone, the pleasure vanished; so that one main end of Dramatic Poesy in its definition, which was to cause delight, was of consequence destroyed.

'In their comedies, the Romans generally borrowed their plots from the Greek poets; and theirs was commonly a little girl stolen or wandered from her parents, brought back unknown to the same city, there got with child by some lewd young fellow, who, by the help of his servant, cheats his father; and when her time comes, to cry *Juno Lucina, fer opem,*[21] one or other sees a little box or cabinet which was carried away with her, and so discovers her to her friends, if some god do not prevent, by coming down in a machine, and take the thanks of it to himself.

'By the plot you may guess much of the characters of the persons. An old father, who would willingly, before he dies, see his son well married; his debauched son, kind in his nature to his wench, but miserably in want of money; a servant or slave, who has so much wit to strike in with him, and help to dupe his father; a braggadochio captain, a parasite, and a lady of pleasure.

'As for the poor honest maid, whom all the story is built upon, and who ought to be one of the principal actors in the play, she is commonly a mute in it: she has the breeding of the old Elizabeth way, for maids to be seen and not to be heard; and it is enough you know she is willing to be married, when the fifth act requires it.

'These are plots built after the Italian mode of houses; you see through them all at once: the characters are indeed the imitations of Nature, but so narrow, as if they had imitated only an eye or an hand, and did not dare to venture on the lines of a face, or the proportion of a body.

'But in how strait a compass soever they have bounded their

20 "Cooked capon."

21 "Juno Lucina, help me" (Terence, *Woman of Andros* 473).

plots and characters, we will pass it by, if they have regularly
pursued them, and perfectly observed those three Unities of
Time, Place, and Action; the knowledge of which you say
is derived to us from them. But in the first place give me
leave to tell you, that the Unity of Place, however it might be
practised by them, was never any of their rules: we neither
find it in Aristotle, Horace, or any who have written of it, till
in our age the French poets made it a precept of the stage.
The Unity of Time, even Terence himself (who was the best
and most regular of them) has neglected: his *Heautonti-
morumenos,* or *Self-Punisher,* takes up visibly two days; therefore, says Scaliger,[22] the two first acts concluding the first day
were acted overnight; the three last on the ensuing day; and
Euripides, in tying himself to one day, has committed an
absurdity never to be forgiven him; for in one of his
tragedies [23] he has made Theseus go from Athens to Thebes,
which was about forty English miles, under the walls of it to
give battle, and appear victorious in the next act; and yet,
from the time of his departure to the return of the Nuntius,
who gives the relation of his victory, Aethra and the Chorus
have but thirty-six verses; that is not for every mile a verse.

'The like error is as evident in Terence his *Eunuch,* when
Laches, the old man, enters in a mistake the house of Thais;
where, betwixt his exit and the entrance of Pythias, who comes
to give an ample relation of the garboyles he has raised within,
Parmeno, who was left upon the stage, has not above five lines
to speak. *C'est bien employer un temps si court,*[24] says the
French poet, who furnished me with one of the observations:
and almost all their tragedies will afford us examples of the
like nature.

'   'Tis true, they have kept the continuity, or, as you called it,
liaison des scenes, somewhat better: two do not perpetually

22 Julius Caesar Scaliger (1484–1558), noted Italian scholar.
23 *The Suppliants.*
24 "It is well to use so short a time." The reference here is to the
Troisième discours (1660), a work of dramatic criticism by Pierre Corneille (1606–1684), French playwright.

come in together, talk, and go out together; and other two succeed them, and do the same throughout the act, which the English call by the name of single scenes; but the reason is, because they have seldom above two or three scenes, properly so called, in every act; for it is to be accounted a new scene, not every time the stage is empty; but every person who enters, though to others, makes it so; because he introduces a new business. Now the plots of their plays being narrow, and the persons few, one of their acts was written in a less compass than one of our well-wrought scenes; and yet they are often deficient even in this. To go no further than Terence; you find in the *Eunuch* Antipho entering single in the midst of the third act, after Cremes and Pythias were gone off; in the same play you have likewise Dorias beginning the fourth act alone; and after she has made a relation of what was done at the Soldier's entertainment (which by the way was very in-artificial, because she was presumed to speak directly to the audience, and to acquaint them with what was necessary to be known, but yet should have been so contrived by the poet as to have been told by persons of the drama to one another, and so by them to have come to the knowledge of the people), she quits the stage, and Phaedria enters next, alone likewise: he also gives you an account of himself, and of his returning from the country, in monologue; to which unnatural way of narration Terence is subject in all his plays. In his *Adelphi*, or Brothers, Syrus and Demea enter after the scene was broken by the departure of Sostrata, Geta, and Canthara; and indeed you can scarce look into any of his comedies, where you will not presently discover the same interruption.

'But as they have failed both in laying of their plots, and managing of them, swerving from the rules of their own art by misrepresenting Nature to us, in which they have ill satis-fied one intention of a play, which was delight; so in the in-structive part they have erred worse: instead of punishing vice and rewarding virtue, they have often shown a prosperous wickedness, and an unhappy piety: they have set before us a bloody image of revenge in Medea, and given her dragons to convey her safe from punishment; a Priam and Astyanax murdered, and Cassandra ravished, and the lust and murder ending in the victory of him who acted them: in short, there is no indecorum in any of our modern plays, which if I would excuse, I could not shadow with some authority from the Ancients.

'And one farther note of them let me leave you: tragedies and comedies were not writ then as they are now, promiscuously, by the same person; but he who found his genius bending to the one, never attempted the other way. This is so plain, that I need not instance to you, that Aristophanes, Plautus, Terence, never any of them writ a tragedy; Aeschylus, Euripides, Sophocles, and Seneca, never meddled with comedy: the sock and buskin [25] were not worn by the same poet. Having them so much care to excel in one kind, very little is to be pardoned then, if they miscarried in it; and this would lead me to the consideration of their wit, had not Crites given me sufficient warning not to be too bold in my judgment of it; because, the languages being dead, and many of the customs and little accidents on which it depended lost to us, we are not competent judges of it. But though I grant that here and there we may miss the application of a proverb or a custom, yet a thing well said will be wit in all languages; and though it may lose something in the translation, yet to him who reads it in the original, 'tis still the same: he has an idea of its excellency, though it cannot pass from his mind to any other expression or words than those in which he finds it. When Phaedria, in the *Eunuch*, had a command from his mistress to be absent two days, and, encouraging himself to go through with it, said, *Tandem ego non illa caream, si sit opus, vel totum triduum?* [26] —Parmeno, to mock the softness of his master, lifting up his hands and eyes, cries out, as it were in admiration, *Hui! universum triduum!* [27] the elegancy of which *universum*, though

25 The symbols of comedy and tragedy on the Roman stage.

26 "Shall I not be without her for three days if need be?" (Terence, *Eunuch* 223).

27 "Alas, all of three days" (*ibid.*, 224).

it cannot be rendered in our language, yet leaves an impression on our souls: but this happens seldom in him; in Plautus oftener, who is infinitely too bold in his metaphors and coining words, out of which many times his wit is nothing; which questionless was one reason why Horace falls upon him so severely in those verses:—

> *Sed proavi nostri Plautinos et numeros et*
> *Laudavere sales, nimium patienter utrumque,*
> *Ne dicam stolide.*[28]

For Horace himself was cautious to obtrude a new word on his readers, and makes custom and common use the best measure of receiving it into our writings:

> *Multa renascentur quae nunc cecidere, cadentque*
> *Quae nunc sunt in honore vocabula, si volet usus,*
> *Quem penes arbitrium est, et jus, et norma loquendi.*[29]

'The not observing this rule is that which the world has blamed in our satyrist, Cleveland: to express a thing hard and unnaturally, is his new way of elocution. 'Tis true, no poet but may sometimes use a catachresis: Virgil does it—

> *Mitasque ridenti colocasia fundet acantho—* [30]

in his eclogue of *Pollio;* and in his 7th *Aeneid.*

> *. . . mirantur et undae,*
> *Miratur nemus insuetum fulgentia longe*
> *Scuta virum fluvio pictasque innare carinas.*[31]

And Ovid once so modestly, that he asks leave to do it:

---

[28] "But our ancestors praised the meter and wit of Plautus, praising each too patiently if not foolishly" (*Art of Poetry* 270–272).

[29] "Many words shall be reborn which have now fallen into disuse and many shall fade that are now well regarded, if usage so demands, in whose power rests the decision, law, and rule of speech" (*ibid.,* 70–72).

[30] "The bean will blossom joined with the laughing acanthus" (*Eclogues* IV. 20).

[31] "Woods and the waters marvel at the shining shields and painted ships on the waves" (*Aeneid* VIII. 91–93).

> . . . *quem, si verbo audacia detur,*
> *Haud metuam summi dixisse Palatia caeli:* [32]

calling the court of Jupiter by the name of Augustus his palace; though in another place he is more bold, where he says—*et longas visent Capitolia pompas.*[33] But to do this always, and never be able to write a line without it, though it may be admired by some few pedants, will not pass upon those who know that wit is best conveyed to us in the most easy language; and is most to be admired when a great thought comes dressed in words so commonly received, that it is understood by the meanest apprehensions, as the best meat is the most easily digested: but we cannot read a verse of Cleveland's without making a face at it, as if every word were a pill to swallow: he gives us many times a hard nut to break our teeth, without a kernel for our pains. So that there is this difference betwixt his *Satires* and doctor Donne's; that the one gives us deep thoughts in common language, through rough cadence; the other gives us common thoughts in abstruse words: 'tis true, in some places his wit is independent of his words, as in that of the *Rebel Scot:*

> Had *Cain* been *Scot,* God would have chang'd his doom;
> Not forc'd him wander, but confin'd him home.[34]

'Si sic omnia dixisset! [35] This is wit in all languages: 'tis like Mercury, never to be lost or killed—and so that other—

> For beauty, like white powder, makes no noise,
> And yet the silent hypocrite destroys.[36]

You see, the last line is highly metaphorical, but it is so soft and gentle, that it does not shock us as we read it.

'But, to return from whence I have digressed, to the con-

[32] "If verbal license is permitted, I will not be afraid to call it the imperial palace" (*Metamorphoses* I. 175–176).

[33] "And the Capitol sees long processions" (*ibid.*, 561).

[34] Cleveland, "Rebel Scot," 63–64.

[35] "If only he had spoken everything thus!" (Juvenal, *Satires* X. 123–124).

[36] Cleveland, "Rupertismus," 39–40.

sideration of the Ancients' writing, and their wit; of which by this time you will grant us in some measure to be fit judges. Though I see many excellent thoughts in Seneca, yet he of them who had a genius most proper for the stage, was Ovid; he had a way of writing so fit to stir up a pleasing admiration and concernment, which are the objects of a tragedy, and to show the various movements of a soul combating betwixt two different passions, that, had he lived in our age, or in his own could have writ with our advantages, no man but must have yielded to him; and therefore I am confident the *Medea* is none of his: for, though I esteem it for the gravity and sententiousness of it, which he himself concludes to be suitable to a tragedy—*Omne genus scripti gravitate tragaedia vincit* [37] —yet it moves not my soul enough to judge that he, who in the epic way wrote things so near the drama as the story of Myrrha, of Caunus and Biblis, and the rest, should stir up no more concernment where he most endeavoured it. The master-piece of Seneca I hold to be that scene in the *Troades,* where Ulysses is seeking for Astyanax to kill him; there you see the tenderness of a mother so represented in Andromache, that it raises compassion to a high degree in the reader, and bears the nearest resemblance of any thing in their tragedies to the excellent scenes of passion in Shakespeare, or in Fletcher: for love-scenes, you will find few among them; their tragic poets dealt not with that soft passion, but with lust, cruelty, revenge, ambition, and those bloody actions they produced; which were more capable of raising horror than compassion in an audience: leaving love untouched, whose gentleness would have tempered them, which is the most frequent of all the passions, and which being the private concernment of every person, is soothed by viewing its own image in a public entertainment.

'Among their comedies, we find a scene or two of tenderness, and that where you would least expect it, in Plautus; but to speak generally, their lovers say little, when they see each

[37] "Tragedy excels every kind of writing in seriousness" (Ovid, *Tristia* II. 381).

other, but *anima mea, vita mea:* ζωη καὶ ψυχή,[38] as the women
in Juvenal's time used to cry out in the fury of their kindness:
then indeed to speak sense were an offence. Any sudden gust
of passion (as an extasy of love in an unexpected meeting)
cannot be better expressed than in a word and a sigh, breaking
one another. Nature is dumb on such occasions; and to make
her speak, would be to represent her unlike herself. But there
are a thousand other concernments of lovers, as jealousies,
complaints, contrivances, and the like, where not to open their
minds at large to each other, were to be wanting to their own
love, and to the expectation of the audience; who watch the
movements of their minds, as much as the changes of their
fortunes. For the imaging of the first is properly the work of
the poet; the latter he borrows of the historian.'

Eugenius was proceeding in that part of his discourse, when
Crites interrupted him. 'I see,' said he, 'Eugenius and I are
never like to have this question decided betwixt us; for he
maintains the Moderns have acquired a new perfection in
writing; I can only grant they have altered the mode of it.
Homer described his heroes men of great appetites, lovers
of beef broiled upon the coals, and good fellows; contrary to
the practice of the French Romances, whose heroes neither eat,
nor drink, nor sleep, for love. Virgil makes Aeneas a bold
avower of his own virtues:

> *Sum pius Aeneas, fama super aethera notus;* [39]

which in the civility of our poets is the character of a fan-
faron or Hector: for with us the knight takes occasion to walk
out, or sleep, to avoid the vanity of telling his own story, which
the trusty squire is ever to perform for him. So in their love-
scenes, of which Eugenius spoke last, the Ancients were more
hearty, we more talkative: they writ love as it was then the
mode to make it; and I will grant thus much to Eugenius,
that perhaps one of their poets, had he lived in our age, *si*

[38] "My soul, my life" (Juvenal, *Satires* VI. 195).

[39] "I am the loyal Aeneas, whose fame is known everywhere" (*Aeneid*
I. 378–379).

foret hoc nostrum fato delapsus in aevum (as Horace says of Lucilius),[40] he had altered many things; not that they were not as natural before, but that he might accommodate himself to the age he lived in. Yet in the mean time, we are not to conclude any thing rashly against those great men, but preserve to them the dignity of masters, and give that honour to their memories, *quos Libitina sacravit*,[41] part of which we expect may be paid to us in future times.'

This moderation of Crites, as it was pleasing to all the company, so it put an end to that dispute; which Eugenius, who seemed to have the better of the argument, would urge no farther: but Lisideius, after he had acknowledged himself of Eugenius his opinion concerning the Ancients, yet told him, he had forborne, till his discourse were ended, to ask him why he preferred the English plays above those of other nations? and whether we ought not to submit our stage to the exactness of our next neighbours?

'Though,' said Eugenius, 'I am at all times ready to defend the honour of my country against the French, and to maintain, we are as well able to vanquish them with our pens, as our ancestors have been with their swords; yet, if you please,' added he, looking upon Neander, 'I will commit this cause to my friend's management; his opinion of our plays is the same with mine: and besides, there is no reason, that Crites and I, who have now left the stage, should re-enter so suddenly upon it; which is against the laws of comedy.'

'If the question had been stated,' replied Lisideius, 'who had writ best, the French or English, forty years ago, I should have been of your opinion, and adjudged the honour to our own nation; but since that time' (said he, turning towards Neander) 'we have been so long together bad Englishmen, that we had not leisure to be good poets. Beaumont, Fletcher, and Johnson (who were only capable of bringing us to that degree of perfection which we have) were just then leaving the

---

[40] "If he had been dropped into our time by fate" (*Satires* I. 10. 68).

[41] "Which Libitina [the goddess of funerals] consecrated" (Horace, *Epistles* II. 1. 49).

world; as if (in an age of so much horror) wit, and those milder studies of humanity, had no farther business among us. But the Muses, who ever follow peace, went to plant in another country: it was then that the great Cardinal of Richelieu began to take them into his protection; and that, by his encouragement, Corneille, and some other Frenchmen, reformed their theatre, which before was as much below ours, as it now surpasses it and the rest of Europe. But because Crites in his discourse for the Ancients has prevented me, by touching upon many rules of the stage which the Moderns have borrowed from them, I shall only, in short, demand of you, whether you are not convinced that of all nations the French have best observed them? In the Unity of Time you find them so scrupulous, that it yet remains a dispute among their poets, whether the artificial day of twelve hours, more or less, be not meant by Aristotle, rather than the natural one of twenty-four; and consequently, whether all plays ought not to be reduced into that compass. This I can testify, that in all their dramas writ within these last twenty years and upwards, I have not observed any that have extended the time to thirty hours: in the Unity of Place they are full as scrupulous; for many of their critics limit it to that very spot of ground where the play is supposed to begin; none of them exceed the compass of the same town or city. The Unity of Action in all plays is yet more conspicuous; for they do not burden them with underplots, as the English do: which is the reason why many scenes of our tragi-comedies carry on a design that is nothing of kin to the main plot; and that we see two distinct webs in a play, like those in ill-wrought stuffs; and two actions, that is, two plays, carried on together, to the confounding of the audience; who, before they are warm in their concernments for one part, are diverted to another; and by that means espouse the interest of neither. From hence likewise it arises, that the one half of our actors are not known to the other. They keep their distances, as if they were Mountagues and Capulets, and seldom begin an acquaintance till the last scene of the fifth act, when they are all to meet upon the stage. There is no theatre in the world has any thing so absurd

as the English tragi-comedy; 'tis a drama of our own invention, and the fashion of it is enough to proclaim it so; here
a course of mirth, there another of sadness and passion, a
third of honour, and fourth a duel: thus, in two hours and
a half, we run through all the fits of Bedlam. The French
affords you as much variety on the same day, but they do it
not so unseasonably, or *mal à propos,* as we: our poets present
you the play and the farce together; and our stages still retain
somewhat of the original civility of the *Red Bull:*

> *Atque ursum et pugiles media inter carmina poscunt.*[42]

The end of tragedies or serious plays, says Aristotle, is to beget
admiration, compassion, or concernment; but are not mirth
and compassion things incompatible? and is it not evident
that the poet must of necessity destroy the former by inter-
mingling of the latter? that is, he must ruin the sole end and
object of his tragedy, to introduce somewhat that is forced
in, and is not of the body of it. Would you not think that
physician mad, who, having prescribed a purge, should immediately order you to take restringents upon it?

'But to leave our plays, and return to theirs. I have noted
one great advantage they have had in the plotting of their
tragedies; that is, they are always grounded upon some known
history: according to that of Horace, *Ex noto fictum carmen
sequar;* [43] and in that they have so imitated the Ancients,
that they have surpassed them. For the Ancients, as was observed before, took for the foundation of their plays some
poetical fiction, such as under that consideration could move
but little concernment in the audience, because they already
knew the event of it. But the French goes farther:

> *Atque ita mentitur, sic veris falsa remiscet,*
> *Primo ne medium, medio ne discrepet imum.*[44]

---

[42] "In the midst of plays they beg for a bear and boxers" (*ibid.,* 185–
186). The Red Bull was a playhouse in St. John Street, Clerkenwell.

[43] "I shall create a poem from a well-known story" (*Art of Poetry* 240).

[44] "He [Homer] so uses fiction and so blends fact with fancy that
neither the middle is inconsistent with the beginning nor the end with
the middle" (*ibid.,* 151–152).

He so interweaves truth with probable fiction, that he puts a pleasing fallacy upon us; mends the intrigues of fate, and dispenses with the severity of history, to reward that virtue which has been rendered to us there unfortunate. Sometimes the story has left the success so doubtful, that the writer is free, by the privilege of a poet, to take that which of two or more relations will best suit with his design: as for example, the death of Cyrus, whom Justin and some others report to have perished in the Scythian war, but Xenophon [45] affirms to have died in his bed of extreme old age. Nay more, when the event is past dispute, even then we are willing to be deceived, and the poet, if he contrives it with appearance of truth, has all the audience of his party; at least during the time his play is acting: so naturally we are kind to virtue, when our own interest is not in question, that we take it up as the general concernment of mankind. On the other side, if you consider the historical plays of Shakespeare, they are rather so many chronicles of kings, or the business many times of thirty or forty years cramped into a representation of two hours and a half; which is not to imitate or paint Nature, but rather to draw her in miniature, to take her in little; to look upon her through the wrong end of a perspective, and receive her images not only much less, but infinitely more imperfect than the life: this, instead of making a play delightful, renders it ridiculous:—

Quodcumque ostendis mihi sic, incredulus odi.[46]

For the spirit of man cannot be satisfied but with truth, or at least verisimility; and a poem is to contain, if not τὰ ἔτυμα, ἐτύμοισιν ὁμοῖα,[47] as one of the Greek poets has expressed it.

'Another thing in which the French differ from us and

---

[45] Cyrus (600?–529 B.C.), emperor of ancient Persia; Justin (or Justinus) (*fl. ca.* 250), Roman historian; Xenophon (434?–355? B.C.), Greek historian and general.

[46] "Whatever you show me thus, disbelieving I detest" (*Art of Poetry* 188).

[47] "True things," "things like the truth" (Hesiod, *Theogony* 27).

from the Spaniards, is, that they do not embarrass, or cumber themselves with too much plot; they only represent so much of a story as will constitute one whole and great action sufficient for a play; we, who undertake more, do but multiply adventures; which, not being produced from one another, as effects from causes, but barely following, constitute many actions in the drama, and consequently make it many plays.

'But by pursuing close one argument, which is not cloyed with many turns, the French have gained more liberty for verse, in which they write; they have leisure to dwell on a subject which deserves it; and to represent the passions (which we have acknowledged to be the poet's work), without being hurried from one thing to another, as we are in the plays of Calderon, which we have seen lately upon our theatres, under the name of Spanish plots. I have taken notice but of one tragedy of ours, whose plot has that uniformity and unity of design in it, which I have commended in the French; and that is *Rollo,* or rather, under the name of Rollo, the story of Bassianus and Geta in Herodian: [48] there indeed the plot is neither large nor intricate, but just enough to fill the minds of the audience, not to cloy them. Besides, you see it founded upon the truth of history, only the time of the action is not reduceable to the strictness of the rules; and you see in some places a little farce mingled, which is below the dignity of the other parts; and in this all our poets are extremely peccant: even Ben Johnson himself, in *Sejanus* and *Catiline,* has given us this oleo [49] of a play, this unnatural mixture of comedy and tragedy; which to me sounds just as ridiculously as the history of David with the merry humours of Golias.[50] In *Sejanus* you make take notice of the scene betwixt Livia and the physician, which is a pleasant satire upon the artificial

48 The reference here is to *The Bloody Brother, or the Tragedy of Rollo Duke of Normandy,* a sensational melodrama first published in 1639, probably the joint work of Chapman, Fletcher, Jonson, and Massinger.

49 *Olla podrida,* a Spanish stew; thus, a hodgepodge.

50 A jovial character in popular medieval literature.

helps of beauty: in *Catiline* you may see the parliament of women; the little envies of them to one another; and all that passes betwixt Curio and Fulvia: scenes admirable in their kind, but of an ill mingle with the rest.

'But I return again to the French writers, who, as I have said, do not burden themselves too much with plot, which has been reproached to them by an *ingenious person* [51] of our nation as a fault; for, he says, they commonly make but one person considerable in a play; they dwell on him, and his concernments, while the rest of the persons are only subservient to set him off. If he intends this by it, that there is one person in the play who is of greater dignity than the rest, he must tax, not only theirs, but those of the Ancients, and which he would be loth to do, the best of ours; for it is impossible but that one person must be more conspicuous in it than any other, and consequently the greatest share in the action must devolve on him. We see it so in the management of all affairs; even in the most equal aristocracy, the balance cannot be so justly poised, but some one will be superior to the rest, either in parts, fortune, interest, or the consideration of some glorious exploit; which will reduce the greatest part of business into his hands.

'But, if he would have us to imagine, that in exalting one character the rest of them are neglected, and that all of them have not some share or other in the action of the play, I desire him to produce any of Corneille's tragedies, wherein every person, like so many servants in a well-governed family, has not some employment, and who is not necessary to the carrying on of the plot, or at least to your understanding it.

'There are indeed some protatick persons [52] in the Ancients, whom they make use of in their plays, either to hear or give the relation: but the French avoid this with great address, making their narrations only to, or by such, who are some way interessed in the main design. And now I am speaking of relations, I cannot take a fitter opportunity to add this in favour

[51] Bishop Thomas Sprat (1635–1713).
[52] Persons involved in the introductory section of a play.   *protasis*

of the French, that they often use them with better judgment and more *à propos* than the English do. Nor that I commend narrations in general—but there are two sorts of them. One, of those things which are antecedent to the play, and are related to make the conduct of it more clear to us. But 'tis a fault to choose such subjects for the stage as will force us on that rock, because we see they are seldom listened to by the audience, and that is many times the ruin of the play; for, being once let pass without attention, the audience can never recover themselves to understand the plot: and indeed it is somewhat unreasonable that they should be put to so much trouble, as that, to comprehend what passes in their sight, they must have recourse to what was done, perhaps, ten or twenty years ago.

'But there is another sort of relations, that is, of things happening in the action of the play, and supposed to be done behind the scenes; and this is many times both convenient and beautiful; for by it the French avoid the tumult which we are subject to in England, by representing duels, battles, and the like; which renders our stage too like the theatres where they fight prizes. For what is more ridiculous than to represent an army with a drum and five men behind it; all which the hero of the other side is to drive in before him; or to see a duel fought, and one slain with two or three thrusts of the foils, which we know are so blunted, that we might give a man an hour to kill another in good earnest with them.

'I have observed that in all our tragedies, the audience cannot forbear laughing when the actors are to die; it is the most comic part of the whole play. All *passions* may be lively represented on the stage, if to the well-writing of them the actor supplies a good commanded voice, and limbs that move easily, and without stiffness; but there are many *actions* which can never be imitated to a just height: dying especially is a thing which none but a Roman gladiator could naturally perform on the stage, when he did not imitate or represent, but naturally do it; and therefore it is better to omit the representation of it.

'The words of a good writer, which describe it lively, will

make a deeper impression of belief in us than all the actor can persuade us to, when he seems to fall dead before us; as a poet in the description of a beautiful garden, or a meadow, will please our imagination more than the place itself can please our sight. When we see death represented, we are convinced it is but fiction; but when he hear it related, our eyes, the strongest witnesses, are wanting, which might have undeceived us; and we are all willing to favour the sleight, when the plot does not too grossly impose on us. They therefore who imagine these relations would make no concernment in the audience, are deceived, by confounding them with the other, which are of things antecedent to the play: those are made often in cold blood, as I may say, to the audience; but these are warmed with our concernments, which were before awakened in the play. What the philosophers say of motion, that, when it is once begun, it continues of itself, and will do so to eternity, without some stop put to it, is clearly true on this occasion: the soul, being already moved with the characters and fortunes of those imaginary persons, continues going of its own accord; and we are no more weary to hear what becomes of them when they are not on the stage, than we are to listen to the news of an absent mistress. But it is objected, that if one part of the play may be related, then why not all? I answer, some parts of the action are more fit to be represented, some to be related. Corneille says judiciously, that the poet is not obliged to expose to view all particular actions which conduce to the principal: he ought to select such of them to be seen, which will appear with the greatest beauty, either by the magnificence of the show, or the vehemence of passions which they produce, or some other charm which they have in them; and let the rest arrive to the audience by narration. 'Tis a great mistake in us to believe the French present no part of the action on the stage; every alteration or crossing of a design, every new-sprung passion, and turn of it, is a part of the action, and much the noblest, except we conceive nothing to be action till they come to blows; as if the painting of the hero's mind were not more properly the poet's work than the strength of his body. Nor does this anything contradict the opinion of Horace, where he tells us,

> *Segnius irritant animos demissa per aurem,*
> *Quam quae sunt oculis subjecta fidelibus.*

For he says immediately after,

> . . . *Non tamen intus*
> *Digna geri promes in scenam;* multaque *tolles*
> *Ex oculis, quae mox narret facundia praesens.*

Among which many he recounts some:

> *Nec pueros coram populo Medea trucidet,*
> *Aut in avem Progne mutetur, Cadmus in anguem; &c.* [53]

That is, those actions which by reason of their cruelty will cause aversion in us, or by reason of their impossibility, unbelief, ought either wholly to be avoided by a poet, or only delivered by narration. To which we may have to add such as to avoid tumult (as was before hinted), or to reduce the plot into a more reasonable compass of time, or for defect of beauty in them, are rather to be related than presented to the eye. Examples of all these kinds are frequent, not only among the Ancients, but in the best received of our English poets. We find Ben Johnson using them in his *Magnetick Lady,* where one comes out from dinner, and relates the quarrels and disorders of it, to save the undecent appearance of them on the stage, and to abbreviate the story; and this in express imitation of Terence, who had done the same before him in his *Eunuch,* where Pythias makes the like relation of what had happened within at the Soldier's entertainment. The relations likewise of Sejanus's death, and the prodigies before it, are

---

[53] "What we hear with our ears moves us less deeply than what we see with our eyes.

". . . You ought not to bring onto the stage what ought to be done off it; many things ought to be kept from the eyes and recounted with vivid immediacy.

"Medea should not cut up her children in front of the audience, nor should Procne be turned into a bird, nor Cadmus into a serpent" (*Art of Poetry* 180–187).

remarkable; the one of which was hid from sight, to avoid the horror and tumult of the representation; the other, to shun the introducing of things impossible to be believed. In that excellent play, *The King and no King,* Fletcher goes yet farther; for the whole unravelling of the plot is done by narration in the fifth act, after the manner of the Ancients; and it moves great concernment in the audience, though it be only a relation of what was done many years before the play. I could multiply other instances, but these are sufficient to prove that there is no error in choosing a subject which requires this sort of narrations; in the ill managing of them, there may.

'But I find I have been too long in this discourse, since the French have many other excellencies not common to us; as that you never see any of their plays end with a conversion, or simple change of will, which is the ordinary way which our poets use to end theirs. It shows little art in the conclusion of a dramatic poem, when they who have hindered the felicity during the four acts, desist from it in the fifth, without some powerful cause to take them off; and though I deny not but such reasons may be found, yet it is a path that is cautiously to be trod, and the poet is to be sure he convinces the audience that the motive is strong enough. As for example, the conversion of the Usurer in *The Scornful Lady*,[54] seems to me a little forced; for, being an Usurer, which implies a lover of money to the highest degree of covetousness (and such the poet has represented him), the account he gives for the sudden change is, that he has been duped by the wild young fellow; which in reason might render him more wary another time, and make him punish himself with harder fare and coarser clothes, to get it up again: but that he should look on it as a judgment, and so repent, we may expect to hear of in a sermon, but I should never endure it in a play.

'I pass by this; neither will I insist on the care they take, that no person after his first entrance shall ever appear, but the business which brings him upon the stage shall be evident;

[54] A play by Beaumont and Fletcher, performed in 1611 and published in 1619.

which, if observed, must needs render all the events in the play more natural; for there you see the probability of every accident, in the cause that produced it; and that which appears chance in the play, will seem so reasonable to you, that you will there find it almost necessary: so that in the exits of the actors you have a clear account of their purpose and design in the next entrance (though, if the scene be well wrought, the event will commonly deceive you), for there is nothing so absurd, says Corneille, as for an actor to leave the stage, only because he has no more to say.

'I should now speak of the beauty of their rhyme, and the just reason I have to prefer that way of writing in tragedies before ours in blank-verse; but because it is partly received by us, and therefore not altogether peculiar to them, I will say no more of it in relation to their plays. For our own, I doubt not but it will exceedingly beautify them; and I can see but one reason why it should not generally obtain, that is, because our poets write so ill in it. This indeed may prove a more prevailing argument than all others which are used to destroy it, and therefore I am only troubled when great and judicious poets, and those who are acknowledged such, have writ or spoke against it: as for others, they are to be answered by that one sentence of an ancient author: *Sed ut primo ad consequendos eos quos priores ducimus, accendimur, ita ubi aut praeteriri, aut aequari eos posse desperavimus, studium cum spe senescit: quod, scilicet, assequi non potest, sequi desinit; . . . praeteritoque eo in quo eminere non possumus, aliquid in quo nitamur, conquirimus.'* [55]

Lisideius concluded in this manner; and Neander, after a little pause, thus answered him:

'I shall grant Lisideius, without much dispute, a great part of what he has urged against us; for I acknowledge that the

[55] "For just as we are led to follow those whom we consider most worthy, so when we give up trying to surpass or equal them, our eagerness and hope lessen; because what it cannot attain, it ceases to follow. . . . And when what we cannot surpass is over, we search for something else for which to aspire" (Velleius Paterculus, *Res gestae divi augusti* [*Historia romana*] I. 17. 7).

French contrive their plots more regularly, and observe the laws of comedy, and decorum of the stage (to speak generally), with more exactness than the English. Farther, I deny not but he has taxed us justly in some irregularities of ours, which he has mentioned; yet, after all, I am of opinion that neither our faults nor their virtues are considerable enough to place them above us.

'For the lively imitation of Nature being in the definition of a play, those which best fulfill that law ought to be esteemed superior to the others. 'Tis true, those beauties of the French poesy are such as will raise perfection higher where it is, but are not sufficient to give it where it is not: they are indeed the beauties of a statue, but not of a man, because not animated with the soul of Poesy, which is imitation of humour and passions: and this Lisideius himself, or any other, however biassed to their party, cannot but acknowledge, if he will either compare the humours of our comedies, or the characters of our serious plays, with theirs. He that will look upon theirs which have been written till these last ten years, or thereabouts, will find it an hard matter to pick out two or three passable humours amongst them. Corneille himself, their arch-poet, what has he produced except *The Liar,* and you know how it was cried up in France; but when it came upon the English stage, though well translated, and that part of Dorant acted to so much advantage by Mr. Hart [56] as I am confident it never received in its own country, the most favourable to it would not put it in competition with many of Fletcher's or Ben Johnson's. In the rest of Corneille's comedies you have little humour; he tells you himself, his way is, first to show two lovers in good intelligence with each other; in the working up of the play to embroil them by some mistake, and in the latter end to clear it, and reconcile them.

'But of late years Molière, the younger Corneille,[57] Qui-

[56] Charles Hart (d. 1683), a popular seventeenth–century actor.

[57] Thomas Corneille (1625–1709), French playwright and brother of Pierre Corneille.

nault,[58] and some others, have been <u>imitating afar</u> off the quick turns and graces of the English stage. They have mixed their serious plays with mirth, like our tragi-comedies, since the death of Cardinal Richelieu; which Lisideius and many others not observing, have commended that in them for a virtue which they themselves no longer practice. Most of their new plays are, like some of ours, derived from the Spanish novels. There is scarce one of them without a veil, and a trusty Diego, who drolls much after the rate of the *Adventures*.[59] But their humours, if I may grace them with that name, are so thin-sown, that never above one of them comes up in any play. I dare take upon me to find more variety of them in some one play of Ben Johnson's, than in all theirs together; as he who has seen *The Alchymist, The Silent Woman,* or *Bartholomew Fair,* cannot but acknowledge with me.

'I grant the French have performed what was possible on the ground-work of the Spanish plays; what was pleasant before, they have made regular: but there is not above one good play to be writ on all those plots; they are too much alike to please often; which we need not the experience of our own stage to justify. As for their new way of mingling mirth with serious plot, I do not, with Lisideius, condemn the thing, though I cannot approve their manner of doing it. He tells us, we cannot so speedily recollect ourselves after a scene of great passion and concernment, as to pass to another of mirth and humour, and to enjoy it with any relish: but why should he imagine the soul of man more heavy than his senses? Does not the eye pass from an unpleasant object to a pleasant in a much shorter time than is required to this? and does not the unpleasantness of the first commend the beauty of the latter? The old rule of logic might have convinced him, that contraries, when placed near, set off each other. A continued gravity keeps the spirit too much bent; we must re-

---

58 Philippe Quinault (1635–1688), a dramatist.
59 The humorous servant in Sir Samuel Tuke's adaptation from the Spanish of *The Adventures of Five Hours* (1663).

fresh it sometimes, as we bait in a journey, that we may go on with greater ease. A scene of mirth, mixed with tragedy, has the same effect upon us which our music has betwixt the acts; and that we find a relief to us from the best plots and language of the stage, if the discourses have been long. I must therefore have stronger arguments, ere I am convinced that compassion and mirth in the same subject destroy each other; and in the mean time cannot but conclude, to the honour of our nation, that we have invented, increased, and perfected a more pleasant way of writing for the stage, than was ever known to the ancients or moderns of any nation, which is tragi-comedy.

'And this leads me to wonder why Lisideius and many others should cry up the barrenness of the French plots, above the variety and copiousness of the English. Their plots are single; they carry on one design, which is pushed forward by all the actors, every scene in the play contributing and moving towards it. Our plays, besides the main design, have underplots or by-concernments, of less considerable persons and intrigues, which are carried on with the motion of the main plot: just as they say the orb of the fixed stars, and those of the planets, though they have motions of their own, are whirled about by the motion of the *Primum Mobile,* in which they are contained.[60] That similitude expresses much of the English stage; for if contrary motions may be found in nature to agree; if a planet can go east and west at the same time, one way by virtue of his own motion, the other by the force of the First Mover, it will not be difficult to imagine how the under-plot, which is only different, not contrary to the great design, may naturally be conducted along with it.

'Eugenius has already shown us, from the confession of the French poets, that the Unity of Action is sufficiently preserved, if all the imperfect actions of the play are conducing to the main design; but when those petty intrigues of a play are so

[60] Dryden here refers to the old Ptolemaic astronomy, in which the Primum Mobile was the sphere beyond the sphere of the fixed stars, which provides motion from east to west for the eight lower spheres.

ill ordered, that they have no coherence with the other, I must grant that Lisideius has reason to tax that want of due connexion; for co-ordination in a play is as dangerous and unnatural as in a state. In the mean time he must acknowledge, our variety, if well ordered, will afford a greater pleasure to the audience.

'As for his other argument, that by pursuing one single theme they gain an advantage to express and work up the passions, I wish any example he could bring from them would make it good; for I confess their verses are to me the coldest I have ever read. Neither, indeed, it is possible for them, in the way they take, so to express passion, as that the effects of it should appear in the concernment of an audience, their speeches being so many declamations, which tire us with the length; so that instead of persuading us to grieve for their imaginary heroes, we are concerned for our own trouble, as we are in the tedious visits of bad company; we are in pain till they are gone. When the French stage came to be reformed by Cardinal Richelieu, those long harangues were introduced, to comply with the gravity of a churchman. Look upon the *Cinna* and the *Pompey;* they are not so properly to be called plays, as long discourses of reason of state; and *Polieucte* [61] in matters of religion is as solemn as the long stops upon our organs. Since that time it is grown into a custom, and their actors speak by the hour-glass, as our parsons do; nay, they account it the grace of their parts, and think themselves disparaged by the poet, if they may not twice or thrice in a play entertain the audience with a speech of an hundred or two hundred lines. I deny not but this may suit well enough with the French; for as we, who are a more sullen people, come to be diverted at our plays, so they, who are of an airy and gay temper, come thither to make themselves more serious: and this I conceive to be one reason why comedy is more pleasing to us, and tragedies to them. But to speak generally: it cannot be denied that short speeches and replies are more apt to move the passions and beget concernment in us, than the

[61] *Cinna, Pompey,* and *Polyeucte* are plays of Pierre Corneille.

other; for it is unnatural for any one in a gust of passion to speak long together, or for another in the same condition to suffer him, without interruption. Grief and passion are like floods raised in little brooks by a sudden rain; they are quickly up; and if the concernment be poured unexpectedly in upon us, it overflows us: but a long sober shower gives them leisure to run out as they came in, without troubling the ordinary current. As for Comedy, repartee is one of its chiefest graces; the greatest pleasure of the audience is a chace of wit, kept up on both sides, and swiftly managed. And this our forefathers, if not we, have had in Fletcher's plays, to a much higher degree of perfection than the French poets can arrive at.

'There is another part of Lisideius his discourse, in which he has rather excused our neighbours, than commended them; that is, for aiming only to make one person considerable in their plays. 'Tis very true what he has urged, that one character in all plays, even without the poet's care, will have advantage of all the others; and that the design of the whole drama will chiefly depend on it. But this hinders not that there may be more shining characters in the play: many persons of a second magnitude, nay, some so very near, so almost equal to the first, that greatness may be opposed to greatness, and all the persons be made considerable, not only by their quality, but their action. 'Tis evident that the more the persons are, the greater will be the variety of the plot. If then the parts are managed so regularly, that the beauty of the whole be kept entire, and that the variety become not a perplexed and confused mass of accidents, you will find it infinitely pleasing to be led in a labyrinth of design, where you see some of your way before you, yet discern not the end till you arrive at it. And that all this is practicable. I can produce for examples many of our English plays: as *The Maid's Tragedy, The Alchymist, The Silent Woman:* [62] I was going to have named *The Fox*, but that the unity of design seems not ex-

[62] *The Maid's Tragedy* was written by Beaumont and Fletcher, the other plays by Ben Jonson.

actly observed in it; for there appear two actions in the play; the first naturally ending with the fourth act; the second forced from it in the fifth: which yet is the less to be condemned in him, because the disguise of Volpone, though it suited not with his character as a crafty or covetous person, agreed well enough with that of a voluptuary; and by it the poet gained the end he aimed at, the punishment of vice, and the reward of virtue, which that disguise produced. So that to judge equally of it, it was an excellent fifth act, but not so naturally proceeding from the former.

'But to leave this, and pass to the latter part of Lisideius his discourse, which concerns relations: I must acknowledge with him, that the French have reason when they hide that part of the action which would occasion too much tumult on the stage, and choose rather to have it made known by narration to the audience. Farther, I think it very convenient, for the reasons he has given, that all incredible actions were removed; but, whether custom has so insinuated itself into our countrymen, or nature has so formed them to fierceness, I know not; but they will scarcely suffer combats and other objects of horror to be taken from them. And indeed, the indecency of tumults is all which can be objected against fighting: for why may not our imagination as well suffer itself to be deluded with the probability of it, as with any other thing in the play? For my part, I can with as great ease persuade myself that the blows which are struck, are given in good earnest, as I can, that they who strike them are kings or princes, or those persons which they represent. For objects of incredibility, I would be satisfied from Lisideius, whether we have any so removed from all appearance of truth, as are those of Corneille's *Andromede;* a play which has been frequented the most of any he has writ. If the Perseus, or the son of an heathen god, the Pegasus, and the Monster, were not capable to choke a strong belief, let him blame any representation of ours hereafter. Those indeed were objects of delight; yet the reason is the same as to the probability: for he makes it not a Ballette or masque, but a play, which is to resemble truth. But for death, that it ought not to be represented, I have, besides the arguments alleged by Lisideius, the authority of Ben Johnson, who has forborn it in his tragedies; for both the death of Sejanus and Catiline are related: though in the latter I cannot but observe one irregularity of that great poet; he has removed the scene in the same act from Rome to Catiline's army, and from thence again to Rome; and besides, has allowed a very inconsiderable time, after Catiline's speech, for the striking of the battle, and the return of Petreius, who is to relate the event of it to the senate: which I should not animadvert on him, who was otherwise a painful observer of τὸ πρέπον, or the *decorum* of the stage, if he had not used extreme severity in his judgment on the incomparable Shakespeare for the same fault. To conclude on this subject of relations; if we are to be blamed for showing too much of the action, the French are as faulty for discovering too little of it: a mean betwixt both should be observed by every judicious writer, so as the audience may neither be left unsatisfied by not seeing what is beautiful, or shocked by beholding what is either incredible or undecent.

'I hope I have already proved in this discourse, that though we are not altogether so punctual as the French, in observing the laws of Comedy, yet our errors are so few, and little, and those things wherein we excel them so considerable, that we ought of right to be preferred before them. But what will Lisideius say, if they themselves acknowledge they are too strictly tied up by those laws, for breaking which he has blamed the English? I will allege Corneille's words, as I find them in the end of his Discourse of the Three Unities: *Il est facile aux speculatifs d'estre severes, &c.* " 'Tis easy for speculative persons to judge severely; but if they would produce to public view ten or twelve pieces of this nature, they would perhaps give more latitude to the rules than I have done, when, by experience, they had known how much we are bound up and constrained by them, and how many beauties of the stage they banished from it." To illustrate a little what he has said: by their servile observations of the Unities of

Time and Place, and integrity of scenes, they have brought
on themselves that dearth of plot, and narrowness of imagination, which may be observed in all their plays. How many
beautiful accidents might naturally happen in two or three
days, which cannot arrive with any probability in the compass
of twenty-four hours? There is time to be allowed also for maturity of design, which, amongst great and prudent persons,
such as are often represented in Tragedy, cannot, with any
likelihood of truth, be brought to pass at so short a warning.
Farther; by tying themselves strictly to the Unity of Place, and
unbroken scenes, they are forced many times to omit some
beauties which cannot be shown where the act began; but
might, if the scene were interrupted, and the stage cleared for
the persons to enter in another place; and therefore the
French poets are often forced upon absurdities; for if the act
begins in a chamber, all the persons in the play must have
some business or other to come thither, or else they are not
shown that act; and sometimes their characters are very un-
fitting to appear there. As, suppose it were the king's bed-
chamber; yet the meanest man in the tragedy must come and
dispatch his business there, rather than in the lobby or court-
yard (which is fitter for him), for fear the stage should be
cleared, and the scenes broken. Many times they fall by it in a
greater inconvenience; for they keep their scenes unbroken,
and yet change the place; as in one of their newest plays,[63]
where the act begins in the street. There a gentleman is to
meet his friend; he sees him with his man, coming out from
his father's house; they talk together, and the first goes out:
the second, who is a lover, has made an appointment with his
mistress; she appears at the window, and then we are to
imagine the scene lies under it. This gentleman is called away,
and leaves his servant with his mistress; presently her father
is heard from within; the young lady is afraid the servingman
should be discovered, and thrusts him in through a door,
which is supposed to be her closet. After this, the father enters

[63] Dryden here and in the following lines refers to Thomas Corneille's
L'amour à la mode (1651).

to the daughter, and now the scene is in a house; for he is seeking from one room to another for this poor Philipin, or French Diego, who is heard from within, drolling and breaking many a miserable conceit upon his sad condition. In this ridiculous manner the play goes on, the stage being never empty all the while: so that the street, the window, the houses, and the closet, are made to walk about, and the persons to stand still. Now what, I beseech you, is more easy than to write a regular French play, or more difficult than write an irregular English one, like those of Fletcher, or of Shakespeare?

'If they content themselves, as Corneille did, with some flat design, which, like an ill riddle, is found out ere it be half proposed, such plots we can make every way regular, as easily as they; but whene'er they endeavour to rise to any quick turns and counterturns of plot, as some of them have attempted, since Corneille's plays have been less in vogue, you see they write as irregularly as we, though they cover it more speciously. Hence the reason is perspicuous, why no French plays, when translated, have, or ever can succeed on the English stage. For, if you consider the plots, our own are fuller of variety; if the writing, ours are more quick and fuller of spirit; and therefore 'tis a strange mistake in those who decry the way of writing plays in verse, as if the English therein imitated the French. We have borrowed nothing from them; our plots are weaved in English looms: we endeavour therein to follow the variety and greatness of characters which are derived to us from Shakespeare and Fletcher; the copiousness and well-knitting of the intrigues we have from Johnson; and for the verse itself we have English precedents of elder date than any of Corneille's plays. Not to name our old comedies before Shakespeare, which were all writ in verse of six feet, or Alexandrines, such as the French now use, I can show in Shakespeare, many scenes of rhyme together, and the like in Ben Johnson's tragedies: in *Catiline* and *Sejanus* sometimes thirty or forty lines, I mean besides the Chorus, or the monologues; which, by the way, showed Ben no enemy to this way of writing, especially if you look upon his *Sad Shepherd,* which goes sometimes on rhyme, sometimes on blank verse, like an horse who eases himself on trot and amble. You find him likewise commending Fletcher's pastoral of *The Faithful Shepherdess,* which is for the most part rhyme, though not refined to that purity to which it hath since been brought. And these examples are enough to clear us from a servile imitation of the French.

'But to return from whence I have digressed: I dare boldly affirm these two things of the English drama; First, that we have many plays of ours as regular as any of theirs, and which, besides, have more variety of plot and characters; and secondly, that in most of the irregular plays of Shakespeare or Fletcher (for Ben Johnson's are for the most part regular) there is a more masculine fancy and greater spirit in the writing, than there is in any of the French. I could produce, even in Shakespeare's and Fletcher's works, some plays which are almost exactly formed; as *The Merry Wives of Windsor,* and *The Scornful Lady:* but because (generally speaking) Shakespeare, who writ first, did not perfectly observe the laws of Comedy, and Fletcher, who came nearer to perfection, yet through carelessness made many faults; I will take the pattern of a perfect play from Ben Johnson, who was a careful and learned observer of the dramatic laws, and from all his comedies I shall select *The Silent Woman;* of which I will make a short examen, according to those rules which the French observe.'

As Neander was beginning to examine *The Silent Woman,* Eugenius, looking earnestly upon him; 'I beseech you, Neander,' said he, 'gratify the company, and me in particular, so far, as before you speak of the play, to give us a character of the author; and tell us frankly your opinion, whether you do not think all writers, both French and English, ought to give place to him.'

'I fear,' replied Neander, 'that in obeying your commands I shall draw a little envy on myself. Besides, in performing them, it will be first necessary to speak somewhat of Shakespeare and Fletcher, his rivals in poesy; and one of them, in my opinion, at least his equal, perhaps his superior.

'To begin, then, with Shakespeare. He was the man who of all modern, and perhaps ancient poets, had the largest and most comprehensive soul. All the images of Nature were still present to him, and he drew them, not laboriously, but luckily; when he describes any thing, you more than see it, you feel it too. Those who accuse him to have wanted learning, give him the greater commendation: he was naturally learn'd; he needed not the spectacles of books to read Nature; he looked inwards, and found her there. I cannot say he is every where alike; were he so, I should do him injury to compare him with the greatest of mankind. He is many times flat, insipid; his comic wit degenerating into clenches, his serious swelling into bombast. But he is always great, when some great occasion is presented to him; no man can say he ever had a fit subject for his wit, and did not then raise himself as high above the rest of poets,

Quantum lenta solent inter viburna cupressi.[64]

The consideration of this made Mr. Hales [65] of Eaton say, that there was no subject of which any poet ever writ, but he would produce it much better treated of in Shakespeare; and however others are now generally preferred before him, yet the age wherein he lived, which had contemporaries with him Fletcher and Johnson, never equalled them to him in their esteem: and in the last King's court, when Ben's reputation was at highest, Sir John Suckling, and with him the greater part of the courtiers, set our Shakespeare far above him.

'Beaumont and Fletcher, of whom I am next to speak, had, with the advantage of Shakespeare's wit, which was their precedent, great natural gifts, improved by study: Beaumont especially being so accurate a judge of plays, that Ben John-

---

[64] "As do cypresses among pliant shrubs" (Virgil, *Eclogues* I. 25).

[65] John Hales (1584–1656), a fellow of Eton, who told of being present when Ben Jonson was speaking of Shakespeare's lack of learning.

son, while he lived, submitted all his writings to his censure, and, 'tis thought, used his judgment in correcting, if not contriving, all his plots. What value he had for him, appears by the verses he writ to him; and therefore I need speak no farther of it. The first play that brought Fletcher and him in esteem was their *Philaster:* for before that, they had written two or three very unsuccessfully, as the like is reported of Ben Johnson, before he writ *Every Man in his Humour.* Their plots were generally more regular than Shakespeare's, especially those which were made before Beaumont's death; and they understood and imitated the conversation of gentlemen much better; whose wild debaucheries, and quickness of wit in repartees, no poet can ever paint as they have done. Humour, which Ben Johnson derived from particular persons, they made it not their business to describe: they represented all the passions very lively, but above all, love. I am apt to believe the English language in them arrived to its highest perfection: what words have since been taken in, are rather superfluous than ornamental. Their plays are now the most pleasant and frequent entertainments of the stage; two of theirs being acted through the year for one of Shakespeare's or Johnson's: the reason is, because there is a certain gaiety in their comedies, and pathos in their more serious plays, which suits generally with all men's humours. Shakespeare's language is likewise a little obsolete, and Ben Johnson's wit comes short of theirs.

'As for Johnson, to whose character I am now arrived, if we look upon him while he was himself (for his last plays were but his dotages), I think him the most learned and judicious writer which any theatre ever had. He was a most severe judge of himself, as well as others. One cannot say he wanted wit, but rather that he was frugal of it. In his works you find little to retrench or alter. Wit, and language, and honour also in some measure, we had before him; but something of art was wanting to the Drama, till he came. He managed his strength to more advantage than any who preceded him. You seldom find him making love in any of his scenes, or endeavouring to

move the passions; his genius was too sullen and saturnine to
do it gracefully, especially when he knew he came after those
who had performed both to such an height. Humour was his
proper sphere; and in that he delighted most to represent
mechanic people. He was deeply conversant in the Ancients,
both Greek and Latin, and he borrowed boldly from them:
there is scarce a poet or historian among the Roman authors
of those times whom he has not translated in *Sejanus* and
Catiline. But he has done his robberies so openly, that one
may see he fears not to be taxed by any law. He invades authors like a monarch; and what would be theft in other poets,
is only victory in him. With the spoils of these writers he so
represents old Rome to us, in its rites, ceremonies, and customs, that if one of their poets had written either of his
tragedies, we had seen less of it than in him. If there was any
fault in his language, 'twas that he weaved it too closely and
laboriously, in his serious plays: perhaps too, he did a little
too much Romanize our tongue, leaving the words which he
translated almost as much Latin as he found them: wherein,
though he learnedly followed the idiom of their language, he
did not enough comply with the idiom of ours. If I would
compare him with Shakespeare, I must acknowledge him the
more correct poet, but Shakespeare the greater wit. Shakespeare was the Homer, or father of our dramatic poets; Johnson was the Virgil, the pattern of elaborate writing; I admire
him, but I love Shakespeare. To conclude of him; as he has
given us the most correct plays, so in the precepts which he
has laid down in his *Discoveries,* we have as many and profit-
able rules for perfecting the stage, as any wherewith the
French can furnish us.

'Having thus spoken of the author, I proceed to the examination of his comedy, *The Silent Woman.*

'Examen of the SILENT WOMAN.

'To begin first with the length of the action; it is so far
from exceeding the compass of a natural day, that it takes

not up an artificial one. 'Tis all included in the limits of three hours and an half, which is no more than is required for the presentment on the stage. A beauty perhaps not much observed; if it had, we should not have looked on the Spanish translation of *Five Hours* [66] with so much wonder. The scene of it is laid in London; the latitude of place is almost as little as you can imagine; for it lies all within the compass of two houses, and after the first act, in one. The continuity of scenes is observed more than in any of our plays, except his own *Fox* and *Alchymist*. They are not broken above twice or thrice at most in the whole comedy; and in the two best of Corneille's plays, the *Cid* and *Cinna,* they are interrupted once apiece. The action of the play is entirely one; the end or aim of which is the settling Morose's estate on Dauphine. The intrigue of it is the greatest and most noble of any pure unmixed comedy in any language; you see it in many persons of various characters and humours, and all delightful: as first, Morose, or an old man, to whom all noise but his own talking is offensive. Some who would be thought critics, say this humour of his is forced: but to remove that objection, we may consider him first to be naturally of a delicate hearing, as many are, to whom all sharp sounds are unpleasant; and secondly, we may attribute much of it to the peevishness of his age, or the wayward authority of an old man in his own house, where he may make himself obeyed; and this the poet seems to allude to in his name Morose. Besides this, I am assured from divers persons, that Ben Johnson was actually acquainted with such a man, one altogether as ridiculous as he is here represented. Others say, it is not enough to find one man of such an humour; it must be common to more, and the more common the more natural. To prove this, they instance in the best of comical characters, Falstaff: there are many men resembling him; old, fat, merry, cowardly, drunken, amorous, vain, and lying. But to convince these people, I need but tell them, that humour is the ridiculous extravagance of conversation, wherein one man differs from all others. If then it be common,

[66] See footnote 59, p. 39.

or communicated to many, how differs it from other men's? or what indeed causes it to be ridiculous so much as the singularity of it? As for Falstaff, he is not properly one humour, but a miscellany of humours or images, drawn from so many several men: that wherein he is singular is his wit, or those things he says *praeter expectatum,* unexpected by the audience; his quick evasions, when you imagine him surprised, which, as they are extremely diverting of themselves, so receive a great addition from his person; for the very sight of such an unwieldy old debauched fellow is a comedy alone. And here, having a place so proper for it, I cannot but enlarge somewhat upon this subject of humour into which I am fallen. The ancients had little of it in their comedies; for the τὸ γελοῖον [67] of the Old Comedy, of which Aristophanes was chief, was not so much to imitate a man, as to make the people laugh at some odd conceit, which had commonly somewhat of unnatural or obscene in it. Thus, when you see Socrates brought upon the stage, you are not to imagine him made ridiculous by the imitation of his actions, but rather by making him perform something very unlike himself; something so childish and absurd, as by comparing it with the gravity of true Socrates, makes a ridiculous object for the spectators. In their New Comedy [68] which succeeded, the poets sought indeed to express the ἦθος [69] as in their tragedies the πάθος [70] of mankind. But this ἦθος contained only the general characters of men and manners; as old men, lovers, serving-men, courtezans, parasites, and such other persons as we see in their comedies; all which they made alike: that is, one old man or father, one lover, one courtezan, so like another, as if the first of them had begot the

---

[67] "The laughable."

[68] The New Comedy (fourth century B.C.) substituted depictions of domestic life for the stinging personal satire of the Old Comedy (fifth century B.C.). The New Comedy of Greece was the direct inspiration for the Roman comedy of Plautus and Terence.

[69] "Character."

[70] "Passion."

rest of every sort: *Ex homine hunc natum dicas*.[71] The same custom they observed likewise in their tragedies. As for the French, though they have the word *humeur* among them, yet they have small use of it in their comedies or farces; they being but ill imitations of the *ridiculum,* or that which stirred up laughter in the Old Comedy. But among the English 'tis otherwise: where by humour is meant some extravagant habit, passion, or affection, particular (as I said before) to some one person, by the oddness of which, he is immediately distinguished from the rest of men; which being lively and naturally represented, most frequently begets that malicious pleasure in the audience which is testified by laughter; as all things which are deviations from common customs are ever the aptest to produce it: though by the way this laughter is only accidental, as the person represented is fantastic or bizarre; but pleasure is essential to it, as the limitation of what is natural. The description of these humours, drawn from the knowledge and observation of particular persons, was the peculiar genius and talent of Ben Johnson; to whose play I now return.

'Besides Morose, there are at least nine or ten different characters and humours in *The Silent Woman;* all which persons have several concernments of their own, yet are all used by the poet, to the conducting of the main design to perfection. I shall not waste time in commending the writing of this play; but I will give you my opinion, that there is more wit and acuteness of fancy in it than in any of Ben Johnson's. Besides, that he has here described the conversation of gentlemen in the persons of True-Wit, and his friends, with more gaiety, air, and freedom, than in the rest of his comedies. For the contrivance of the plot, 'tis extreme elaborate, and yet withal easy; for the λύσις, or untying of it, 'tis so admirable, that when it is done, no one of the audience would think the poet could have missed it; and yet it was concealed so much before the last scene, that any other way would sooner have entered into your thoughts. But I dare not take upon me to commend

[71] "You would say he was born of the other man" (Terence, *Eunuch* 460).

the fabric of it, because it is altogether so full of art, that I must unravel every scene in it to commend it as I ought. And this excellent contrivance is still the more to be admired, because 'tis comedy, where the persons are only of common rank, and their business private, not elevated by passions or high concernments, as in serious plays. Here every one is a proper judge of all he sees, nothing is represented but that with which he daily converses: so that by consequence all faults lie open to discovery, and few are pardonable. 'Tis this which Horace has judiciously observed:

> *Creditur, ex medio quia res arcessit, habere*
> *Sudoris minimum; sed habet Comedia tanto*
> *Plus oneris, quanto veniae minus.*[72]

But our poet who was not ignorant of these difficulties, had prevailed himself of all advantages; as he who designs a large leap takes his rise from the highest ground. One of these advantages is that which Corneille has laid down as the greatest which can arrive to any poem, and which he himself could never compass above thrice in all his plays; viz. the making choice of some signal and long-expected day, whereon the action of the play is to depend. This day was that designed by Dauphine for the settling of his uncle's estate upon him; which to compass, he contrives to marry him. That the marriage had been plotted by him long beforehand, is made evident by what he tells True-Wit in the second act, that in one moment he had destroyed what he had been raising many months.

'There is another artifice of the poet, which I cannot here omit, because by the frequent practice of it in his comedies he has left it to us almost as a rule; that is, when he has any character of humour wherein he would show a *coup de Maistre*, or his highest skill, he recommends it to your observation by a pleasant description of it before the person first

---

[72] "It is believed that comedy demands the least effort because it draws its subjects from the ordinary; but the less indulgence it has, the greater work it needs" (Horace, *Epistles* II. 1. 168–170).

appears. Thus, in *Bartholomew Fair* he gives you the pictures of Numps and Cokes, and in this those of Daw, Lafoole, Morose, and the Collegiate Ladies; all which you hear described before you see them. So that before they come upon the stage, you have a longing expectation of them, which prepares you to receive them favourably; and when they are there, even from their first appearance you are so far acqainted with them, that nothing of their humour is lost to you.

'I will observe yet one thing further of this admirable plot; the business of it rises in every act. The second is greater than the first; the third than the second; and so forward to the fifth. There too you see, till the very last scene, new difficulties arising to obstruct the action of the play; and when the audience is brought into despair that the business can naturally be effected, then, and not before, the discovery is made. But that the poet might entertain you with more variety all this while, he reserves some new characters to show you, which he opens not till the second and third act. In the second Morose, Daw, the Barber, and Otter; in the third the Collegiate Ladies: all which he moves afterwards in bywalks, or under-plots, as diversions to the main design, lest it should grow tedious, though they are still naturally joined with it, and somewhere or other subservient to it. Thus, like a skilful chess-player, by little and little he draws out his men, and makes his pawns of use to his greater persons.

'If this comedy and some others of his were translated into French prose (which would now be no wonder to them, since Molière has lately given them plays out of verse, which have not displeased them), I believe the controversy would soon be decided betwixt the two nations, even making them the judges. But we need not call our heroes to our aid; be it spoken to the honour of the English, our nation can never want in any age such who are able to dispute the empire of wit with any people in the universe. And though the fury of a civil war, and power for twenty years together abandoned to a barbarous race of men, enemies of all good learning, had buried the Muses under the ruins of monarchy; yet, with the

restoration of our happiness, we see revived Poesy lifting up
its head, and already shaking off the rubbish which lay so
heavy on it. We have seen since his Majesty's return, many
dramatic poems which yield not to those of any foreign nation,
and which deserve all laurels but the English. I will set aside
flattery and envy: it cannot be denied but we have had some
little blemish either in the plot or writing of all those plays
which have been made within these seven years (and perhaps there is no nation in the world so quick to discern them,
or so difficult to pardon them, as ours): yet if we can persuade
ourselves to use the candour of that poet, who, though the
most severe of critics, has left us this caution by which to
moderate our censures—

> . . . *ubi plura nitent in carmine, non ego paucis*
> *Offendar maculis;* [73]

if, in consideration of their many and great beauties, we can
wink at some slight and little imperfections, if we, I say, can
be thus equal to ourselves, I ask no favour from the French.
And if I do not venture upon any particular judgment of our
late plays, 'tis out of the consideration which an ancient writer
gives me: *vivorum, ut magna admiratio, ita censura diffi-
cilis:* [74] betwixt the extremes of admiration and malice, 'tis
hard to judge uprightly of the living. Only I think it may be
permitted me to say, that as it is no lessening to us to yield
to some plays, and those not many, of our own nation in the
last age, so can it be no addition to pronounce of our present
poets, that they have far surpassed all the Ancients, and the
modern writers of other countries.'

This, my Lord, was the substance of what was then spoke on
that occasion; and Lisideius, I think, was going to reply, when
he was prevented thus by Crites: 'I am confident,' said he,

73 "Where many beauties shine in a poem, I will not be bothered by
little faults" (Horace, *Art of Poetry* 351–352).
74 "Admiration for the living is great, censure is difficult" (Velleius
Paterculus, *Res gestae divi augusti* [*Historia romana*] II. 36. 3).

'that the most material things that can be said have been already urged on either side; if they have not, I must beg of Lisideius that he will defer his answer till another time: for I confess I have a joint quarrel to you both, because you have concluded, without any reason given for it, that rhyme is proper for the stage. I will not dispute how ancient it hath been among us to write this way; perhaps our ancestors knew no better till Shakespeare's time. I will grant it was not altogether left by him, and that Fletcher and Ben Johnson used it frequently in their Pastorals, and sometimes in other plays. Farther, I will not argue whether we received it originally from our own countrymen, or from the French; for that is an inquiry of as little benefit, as theirs who, in the midst of the great Plague, were not so solicitous to provide against it, as to know whether we had it from the malignity of our own air, or by transportation from Holland. I have therefore only to affirm, that it is not allowable in serious plays; for comedies, I find you already concluding with me. To prove this, I might satisfy myself to tell you, how much in vain it is for you to strive against the stream of the people's inclination; the greatest part of which are prepossessed so much with those excellent plays of Shakespeare, Fletcher, and Ben Johnson, which have been written out of rhyme, that except you could bring them such as were written better in it, and those too by persons of equal reputation with them, it will be impossible for you to gain your cause with them, who will still be judges. This it is to which, in fine, all your reasons must submit. The unanimous consent of an audience is so powerful, that even Julius Caesar (as Macrobius reports of him), when he was perpetual dictator, was not able to balance it on the other side. But when Laberius, a Roman Knight, at his request contended in the Mime with another poet, he was forced to cry out, *Etiam favente me victus es, Laberi*.[75] But I will not on this occasion take the advantage of the greater number, but only urge such reasons against rhyme, as I find in the writings

[75] "Even with me beside you, you are defeated, Laberius" (Macrobius, *Saturnalia* II. 7).

of those who have argued for the other way. First then, I am of opinion, that rhyme is unnatural in a play, because dialogue there is presented as the effect of sudden thought: for a play is the imitation of Nature; and since no man without premeditation speaks in rhyme, neither ought he to do it on the stage. This hinders not but the fancy may be there elevated to an higher pitch of thought than it is in ordinary discourse; for there is a probability that men of excellent and quick parts may speak noble things *ex tempore:* but those thoughts are never fettered with the numbers or sound of verse without study, and therefore it cannot be but unnatural to present the most free way of speaking in that which is the most constrained. For this reason, says Aristotle, 'tis best to write tragedy in that kind of verse which is the least such, or which is nearest prose: and this amongst the Ancients was the iambic, and with us is blank verse, or the measure of verse kept exactly without rhyme. These numbers therefore are fittest for a play; the others for a paper of verses, or a poem; blank verse being as much below them, as rhyme is improper for the Drama. And if it be objected that neither are blank verses made *ex tempore,* yet, as nearest nature, they are still to be preferred. But there are two particular exceptions, which many besides myself have had to verse; by which it will appear yet more plainly how improper it is in plays. And the first of them is grounded on that very reason for which some have commended rhyme; they say, the quickness of repartees in argumentative scenes receives an ornament from verse. Now what is more unreasonable than to imagine that a man should not only light upon the wit, but the rhyme too, upon the sudden? This nicking of him who spoke before both in sound and measure, is so great an happiness, that you must at least suppose the persons of your play to be born poets: *Arcades omnes, et cantare pares, et respondere parati:* [76] they must have arrived to the degree of *quicquid conabar*

---

[76] "All the Arcadians, prepared to sing and respond" (Virgil, *Eclogues* VII. 4–5).

dicere [77]—to make verses almost whether they will or no. If they are any thing below this, it will look rather like the design of two, than the answer of one: it will appear that your actors hold intelligence together; that they perform their tricks like fortune-tellers, by confederacy. The hand of art will be too visible in it, against that maxim of all professions, *Ars est celare artem*,[78] that it is the greatest perfection of art to keep itself undiscovered. Nor will it serve you to object, that however you manage it, 'tis still known to be a play; and, consequently, the dialogue of two persons understood to be the labour of one poet. For a play is still an imitation of Nature; we know we are to be deceived, and we desire to be so; but no man ever was deceived but with a probability of truth; for who will suffer a gross lie to be fastened on him? Thus we sufficiently understand, that the scenes which represent cities and countries to us are not really such, but only painted on boards and canvas; but shall that excuse the ill painture or designment of them? Nay, rather ought they not be laboured with so much the more diligence and exactness, to help the imagination? since the mind of man does naturally tend to, and seek after truth; and therefore the nearer any thing comes to the imitation of it, the more it pleases.

'Thus, you see, your rhyme is uncapable of expressing the greatest thoughts naturally, and the lowest it cannot with any grace: for what is more unbefitting the majesty of verse, than to call a servant, or bid a door to shut in rhyme? And yet this miserable necessity you are forced upon. But verse, you say, circumscribes a quick and luxuriant fancy, which would extend itself too far on every subject, did not the labour which is required to well-turned and polished rhyme, set bounds to it. Yet this argument, if granted, would only prove that we may write better in verse, but not more naturally. Neither is it able to evince that; for he who wants judgment to confine his fancy in blank verse, may want it as much in rhyme: and

---

[77] Watson suggests that this is probably a corruption from Ovid, *Tristia* IV. 10. 26.

[78] "It is art to conceal art" (source unidentified).

he who has it will avoid errors in both kinds. Latin verse was as great a confinement to the imagination of those poets, as rhyme to ours; and yet you find Ovid saying too much on every subject. *Nescivit* (says Seneca) *quod bene cessit relinquere:* [79] of which he gives you one famous instance in his description of the deluge:

> *Omnia pontus erat, deerant quoque litora ponto.*
> Now all was sea, nor had that sea a shore.[80]

Thus Ovid's fancy was not limited by verse, and Virgil needed not verse to have bounded his.

'In our own language we see Ben Johnson confining himself to what ought to be said, even in the liberty of blank verse; and yet Corneille, the most judicious of the French poets, is still varying the same sense an hundred ways, and dwelling eternally on the same subject, though confined by rhyme. Some other exceptions I have to verse; but being these I have named are for the most part already public, I conceive it reasonable they should first be answered.'

'It concerns me less than any,' said Neander (seeing he had ended), 'to reply to this discourse; because when I should have proved that verse may be natural in plays, yet I should always be ready to confess, that those which I have written in this kind come short of that perfection which is required. Yet since you are pleased I should undertake this province, I will do it, though with all imaginable respect and deference, both to that person from whom you have borrowed your strongest arguments, and to whose judgment, when I have said all, I finally submit. But before I proceed to answer your objections, I must first remember you, that I exclude all Comedy from my defence; and next that I deny not but blank verse may be also used; and content myself only to assert, that in serious plays where the subject and characters are great, and the plot unmixed with mirth, which might allay or divert these con-

[79] "He did not know how to end when he should have done so" (the elder Seneca, *Controversiae* IX. 5).
[80] Ovid, *Metamorphoses*, I. 292.

cernments which are produced, rhyme is there as natural and more effectual than blank verse.

'And now having laid down this as a foundation—to begin with Crites, I must crave leave to tell him, that some of his arguments against rhyme reach no farther than, from the faults or defects of ill rhyme, to conclude against the use of it in general. May not I conclude against blank verse by the same reason? If the words of some poets who write in it, are either ill chosen, or ill placed, which makes not only rhyme, but all kind of verse in any language unnatural, shall I, for their vicious affectation, condemn those excellent lines of Fletcher, which are written in that kind? Is there any thing in rhyme more constrained than this line in blank verse, *I heaven invoke, and strong resistance make?* where you see both the clauses are placed unnaturally, that is, contrary to the common way of speaking, and that without the excuse of a rhyme to cause it: yet you would think me very ridiculous, if I should accuse the stubbornness of blank verse for this, and not rather the stiffness of the poet. Therefore, Crites, you must either prove that words, though well chosen, and duly placed, yet render not rhyme natural in itself; or that, however natural and easy the rhyme may be, yet it is not proper for a play. If you insist on the former part, I would ask you, what other conditions are required to make rhyme natural in itself, besides an election of apt words, and a right disposing of them? For the due choice of your words expresses your sense naturally, and the due placing them adapts the rhyme to it. If you object that one verse may be made for the sake of another, though both the words and rhyme be apt, I answer, it cannot possibly so fall out; for either there is a dependance of sense betwixt the first line and the second, or there is none: if there be that connection, then in the natural position of the words the latter line must of necessity flow from the former; if there be no dependance, yet still the due ordering of words makes the last line as natural in itself as the other: so that the necessity of a rhyme never forces any but bad or lazy writers to say what they would not otherwise. 'Tis true, there is both care and art required to write in verse. A good poet never concludes upon the first line, till he has sought out such a rhyme as may fit the sense, already prepared to heighten the second: many times the close of the sense falls into the middle of the next verse, or farther off, and he may often prevail himself of the same advantages in English which Virgil had in Latin; he may break off in the hemistich,[81] and begin another line. Indeed, the not observing these two last things, makes plays which are writ in verse so tedious: for though, most commonly, the sense is to be confined to the couplet, yet nothing that does *perpetuo tenore fluere*,[82] run in the same channel, can please always. 'Tis like the murmuring of a stream, which not varying in the fall, causes at first attention, at last drowsiness. Variety of cadences is the best rule; the greatest help to the actors, and refreshment to the audience.

'If then verse may be made natural in itself, how becomes it improper to a play? You say the stage is the representation of Nature, and no man in ordinary conversation speaks in rhyme. But you foresaw when you said this, that it might be answered —neither does any man speak in blank verse, or in measure without rhyme. Therefore you concluded, that which is nearest Nature is still to be preferred. But you took no notice that rhyme might be made as natural as blank verse, by the well placing of the words, &c. All the difference between them, when they are both correct, is, the sound in one, which the other wants; and if so, the sweetness of it, and all the advantage resulting from it, which are handled in the Preface to *The Rival Ladies*, will yet stand good. As for that place of Aristotle, where he says, plays should be writ in that kind of verse which is nearest prose, it makes little for you; blank verse being properly but measured prose. Now measure alone, in any modern language, does not constitute verse; those of the Ancients in Greek and Latin consisted in quantity of words, and a determinate number of feet. But when, by the inundation of the Goths and Vandals into Italy, new lan-

---

[81] Half a poetic verse or line.
[82] Probably based on Cicero, *De oratore* VI. 21.

guages were brought in, and barbarously mingled with the Latin, of which the Italian, Spanish, French, and ours (made out of them and the Teutonic) are dialects, a new way of poesy was practised; new, I say, in those countries, for in all probability it was that of the conquerors in their own nations. This new way consisted in measure or numbers of feet, and rhyme; the sweetness of rhyme, and observation of accent, supplying the place of quantity in words, which could neither exactly be observed by those Barbarians, who knew not the rules of it, neither was it suitable to their tongues, as it had been to the Greek and Latin. No man is tied in modern poesy to observe any farther rule in the feet of his verse, but that they be dissyllables; whether spondee, trochee, or iambic, it matters not; only he is obliged to rhyme. Neither do the Spanish, French, Italian, or Germans, acknowledge at all, or very rarely, any such kind of poesy as blank verse amongst them. Therefore, at most 'tis but a poetic prose, a *sermo pe-destris;* and as such, most fit for comedies, where I acknowl-edge rhyme to be improper. Farther; as to that quotation of Aristotle, our couplet verses may be rendered as near prose as blank verse itself, by using those advantages I lately named, as breaks in a hemistich, or running the sense into another line, thereby making art and order appear as loose and free as nature: or not tying ourselves to couplets strictly, we may use the benefit of the Pindaric way practised in *The Siege of Rhodes;* [83] where the numbers vary, and the rhyme is disposed carelessly, and far from often chiming. Neither is that other advantage of the Ancients to be despised, of changing the kind of verse when they please, with the change of the scene, or some new entrance; for they confine not themselves always to iambics, but extend their liberty to all lyric numbers, and sometimes even to hexameter. But I need not go so far to prove that rhyme, as it succeeds to all other offices of Greek and Latin verse, so especially to this of plays, since the custom of all nations at this day confirms it, all the French, Italian,

[83] An opera and heroic play by Sir William Davenant (1606–1668). It was performed in 1656 and published in 1663.

and Spanish tragedies are generally writ in it; and sure the universal consent of the most civilized parts of the world ought in this, as it doth in other customs, to include the rest.

'But perhaps you may tell me, I have proposed such a way to make rhyme natural, and consequently proper to plays, as is unpracticable; and that I shall scarce find six or eight lines together in any play, where the words are so placed and chosen as is required to make it natural. I answer, no poet need constrain himself at all times to it. It is enough he makes it his general rule; for I deny not but sometimes there may be a greatness in placing the words otherwise; and sometimes they may sound better, sometimes also the variety itself is excuse enough. But if, for the most part, the words be placed as they are in the negligence of prose, it is sufficient to denominate the way practicable; for we esteem that to be such, which in the trial oftener succeeds than misses. And thus far you may find the practice made good in many plays: where you do not, remember still, that if you cannot find six natural rhymes together, it will be as hard for you to produce as many lines in blank verse, even among the greatest of our poets, against which I cannot make some reasonable exception.

'And this, Sir, calls to my remembrance the beginning of your discourse, where you told us we should never find the audience favourable to this kind of writing, till we could produce as good plays in rhyme, as Ben Johnson, Fletcher, and Shakespeare, had writ out of it. But it is to raise envy to the living, to compare them with the dead. They are honoured, and almost adored by us, as they deserve; neither do I know any so presumptuous of themselves as to contend with them. Yet give me leave to say thus much, without injury to their ashes; that not only we shall never equal them, but they could never equal themselves, were they to rise and write again. We acknowledge them our fathers in wit; but they have ruined their estates themselves, before they came to their children's hands. There is scarce an humour, a character, or any kind of plot, which they have not blown upon. All comes sullied or wasted to us: and were they to entertain this age, they could not make so plenteous treatments out of such decayed fortunes. This therefore will be a good argument to us, either not to write at all, or to attempt some other way. There is no bays to be expected in their walks: *tentanda via est, qua me quoque possum tollere humo.*[84]

'This way of writing in verse they have only left free to us; our age is arrived to a perfection in it, which they never knew; and which (if we may guess by what of theirs we have seen in verse, as *The Faithful Shepherdess*, and *Sad Shepherd*)[85] 'tis probable they never could have reached. For the genius of every age is different; and though ours excel in this, I deny not but that to imitate Nature in that perfection which they did in prose, is a greater commendation than to write in verse exactly. As for what you have added, that the people are not generally inclined to like this way; if it were true, it would be no wonder, that betwixt the shaking off an old habit, and the introducing of a new, there should be difficulty. Do we not see them stick to Hopkins' and Sternhold's psalms,[86] and forsake those of David, I mean Sandys[87] his translation of them? If by the people you understand the multitude, the οἱ πολλοί, 'tis no matter what they think; they are sometimes in the right, sometimes in the wrong: their judgment is a mere lottery. *Est ubi plebs recte putat, est ubi peccat.*[88] Horace says it of the vulgar, judging poesy. But if you mean the mixed audience of the populace and the noblesse, I dare confidently affirm that a great part of the latter sort are already favourable to verse; and that no serious plays written since the

84 "A way must be found by which I can raise myself up" (Virgil, *Georgics* III. 8–9).

85 *The Faithful Shepherdess,* the first play by John Fletcher; *The Sad Shepherd,* a pastoral play by Jonson.

86 John Hopkins (d. 1570) and Thomas Sternhold (d. 1549), joint authors of a metrical version of the *Psalms*.

87 George Sandys (1578–1644), known for his *A Paraphrase upon the Psalms of David and upon the Hymnes Dispersed Throughout the Old and New Testaments* (1636), as well as for his translations from Ovid.

88 "It is where the common people think they are right that they are wrong" (*Epistles* II. 1. 63).

King's return have been more kindly received by them, than *The Siege of Rhodes*, the *Mustapha*, *The Indian Queen*, and *Indian Emperor*.[89]

'But I come now to the inference of your first argument. You said the dialogue of plays is presented as the effect of sudden thought, but no man speaks suddenly, or *ex tempore*, in rhyme; and you inferred from thence, that rhyme, which you acknowledge to be proper to epic poesy, cannot equally be proper to dramatic, unless we could suppose all men born so much more than poets, that verses should be made in them, not by them.

'It has been formerly urged by you, and confessed by me, that since no man spoke any kind of verse *ex tempore*, that which was nearest to Nature was to be preferred. I answer you, therefore, by distinguishing betwixt what is nearest to the nature of Comedy, which is the imitation of common persons and ordinary speaking, and what is nearest the nature of a serious play: this last is indeed the representation of Nature, but 'tis Nature wrought up to an higher pitch. The plot, the characters, the wit, the passions, the descriptions, are all exalted above the level of common converse, as high as the imagination of the poet can carry them, with proportion to verisimility. Tragedy, we know, is wont to image to us the minds and fortunes of noble persons, and to portray these exactly; heroic rhyme is nearest Nature, as being the noblest kind of modern verse.

> *Indignatur enim privatis et prope socco*
> *Dignis carminibus narrari coena Thyestae,*[90]

says Horace: and in another place,

> *Effutire leves indigna tragaedia versus.*[91]

[89] *The Siege of Rhodes* by William Davenant; *Mustapha* by Roger Boyle, Earl of Orrery; *The Indian Queen* and *The Indian Emperor* by Dryden.

[90] "The banquet of Thyestes ought not to be recounted in common verses associated with Comedy" (*Art of Poetry* 90–91).

[91] "It is inappropriate for Tragedy to babble in trivial verses" (*ibid.*, 231).

Blank verse is acknowledged to be too low for a poem, nay more, for a paper of verses; but if too low for an ordinary sonnet, how much more for Tragedy, which is by Aristotle, in the dispute betwixt the epic poesy and the dramatic, for many reasons he there alleges, ranked above it?

'But setting this defence aside, your argument is almost as strong against the use of rhyme in poems as in plays; for the epic way is every where interlaced with dialogue, or discoursive scenes; and therefore you must either grant rhyme to be improper there, which is contrary to your assertion, or admit it into plays by the same title which you have given it to poems. For though Tragedy be justly preferred above the other, yet there is a great affinity between them, as may easily be discovered in that definition of a play which Lisideius gave us. The *genus* of them is the same, a just and lively image of human nature, in its actions, passions, and traverses of fortune: so is the end, namely, for the delight and benefit of mankind. The characters and persons are still the same, viz. the greatest of both sorts; only the manner of acquainting us with those actions, passions, and fortunes, is different. Tragedy performs it *viva voce*, or by action, in dialogue; wherein it excels the Epic Poem, which does it chiefly by narration, and therefore is not so lively an image of human nature. However, the agreement betwixt them is such, that if rhyme be proper for one, it must be for the other. Verse, 'tis true, is not the effect of sudden thought; but this hinders not that sudden thought may be represented in verse, since those thoughts are such as must be higher than Nature can raise them without premeditation, especially to a continuance of them, even out of verse; and consequently you cannot imagine them to have been sudden either in the poet or in the actors. A play, as I have said, to be like Nature, is to be set above it; as statues which are placed on high are made greater than the life, that they may descend to the sight in their just proportion.

'Perhaps I have insisted too long on this objection; but the clearing of it will make my stay shorter on the rest. You tell us, Crites, that rhyme appears most unnatural in repartees, or short replies: when he who answers, it being presumed he knew not what the other would say, yet makes up that part of the verse which was left incomplete, and supplies both the sound and measure of it. This, you say, looks rather like the confederacy of two, than the answer of one.

'This, I confess, is an objection which is in every one's mouth, who loves not rhyme: but suppose, I beseech you, the repartee were made only in blank verse, might not part of the same argument be turned against you? for the measure is as often supplied there, as it is in rhyme; the latter half of the hemistich as commonly made up, or a second line subjoined as a reply to the former; which any one leaf in Johnson's plays will sufficiently clear to you. You will often find in the Greek tragedians, and in Seneca, that when a scene grows up into the warmth of repartees, which is the close fighting of it, the latter part of the trimeter is supplied by him who answers; and yet it was never observed as a fault in them by any of the ancient or modern critics. The case is the same in our verse, as it was in theirs; rhyme to us being in lieu of quantity to them. But if no latitude is to be allowed a poet, you take from him not only his licence of *quidlibet audendi*,[92] but you tie him up in a straiter compass than you would a philosopher. This is indeed *Musas colere severiores*.[93] You would have him follow Nature, but he must follow her on foot: you have dismounted him from his Pegasus. But you tell us, this supplying the last half of a verse, or adjoining a whole second to the former, looks more like the design of two, than the answer of one. Supposing we acknowledge it: how comes this confederacy to be more displeasing to you, than in a dance which is well contrived? You see there the united design of many persons to make up one figure: after they have separated themselves in many petty divisions, they rejoin one by one into a gross: the confederacy is plain amongst them, for chance could

92 "Daring anything" (*ibid.*, 10).

93 "To cultivate the more demanding Muses" (Martial, *Epigrams* IX. 11. 17).

never produce any thing so beautiful; and yet there is nothing in it, that shocks your sight. I acknowledge the hand of art appears in repartee, as of necessity it must in all kinds of verse. But there is also the quick and poynant brevity of it (which is an high imitation of Nature in those sudden gusts of passion) to mingle with it; and this, joined with the cadency and sweetness of the rhyme, leaves nothing in the soul of the hearer to desire. 'Tis an art which appears; but it appears only like the shadowings of painture, which being to cause the rounding of it, cannot be absent; but while that is considered, they are lost: so while we attend to the other beauties of the matter, the care and labour of the rhyme is carried from us, or at least drowned in its own sweetness, as bees are sometimes buried in their honey. When a poet has found the repartee, the last perfection he can add to it, is to put it into verse. However good the thought may be, however apt the words in which 'tis couched, yet he finds himself at a little unrest, while rhyme is wanting: he cannot leave it till that comes naturally, and then is at ease, and sits down contented.

'From replies, which are the most elevated thoughts of verse, you pass to the most mean ones, those which are common with the lowest of household conversation. In these, you say, the majesty of verse suffers. You instance in the calling of a servant, or commanding a door to be shut, in rhyme. This, Crites, is a good observation of yours, but no argument: for it proves no more but that such thoughts should be waved, as often as may be, by the address of the poet. But suppose they are necessary in the places where he uses them, yet there is no need to put them into rhyme. He may place them in the beginning of a verse, and break it off, as unfit, when so debased, for any other use; or granting the worst—that they require more room than the hemistich will allow, yet still there is a choice to be made of the best words, and least vulgar (provided they be apt) to express such thoughts. Many have blamed rhyme in general, for this fault, when the poet with a little care might have redressed it. But they do it with no more justice, than if English Poesy should be made ridiculous

for the sake of the Water Poet's rhymes.[94] Our language is
noble, full, and significant; and I know not why he who is
master of it may not clothe ordinary things in it as decently as
the Latin, if we use the same diligence in his choice of words.
Delectus verborum origo est eloquentiae.[95] It was the saying of
Julius Caesar, one so curious in his, that none of them can be
changed but for the worse. One would think, *unlock the door,*
was a thing as vulgar as could be spoken; and yet Seneca could
make it sound high and lofty in his Latin:

> *Reserate clusos regii postes laris.*
> Set wide the palace gates.[96]

'But I turn from this exception, both because it happens
not above twice or thrice in any play that those vulgar
thoughts are used; and then too, were there no other apology
to be made, yet the necessity of them, which is alike in all
kind of writing, may excuse them. Besides that the great
eagerness and precipitation with which they are spoken makes
us rather mind the substance than the dress; that for which
they are spoken, rather than what is spoke. For they are
always the effect of some hasty concernment, and something
of consequence depends on them.

'Thus, Crites, I have endeavoured to answer your objections; it remains only that I should vindicate an argument for
verse, which you have gone about to overthrow. It had formerly been said, that the easiness of blank verse renders the
poet too luxuriant, but that the labour of rhyme bounds and
circumscribes an overfruitful fancy; the sense there being commonly confined to the couplet, and the words so ordered that
the rhyme naturally follows them, not they the rhyme. To
this you answered, that it was no argument to the question in
hand; for the dispute was not which way a man may write

94 John Taylor (1578–1653), a popular poet.
95 "Choice of words is the beginning of eloquence" (Cicero, *Brutus*
LXXII. 253).
96 *Hippolytus* 863.

best, but which is most proper for the subject on which he writes.

'First, give me leave, Sir, to remember you, that the argument against which you raised this objection, was only secondary: it was built on this hypothesis, that to write in verse was proper for serious plays. Which supposition being granted (as it was briefly made out in that discourse, by showing how verse might be made natural), it asserted, that this way of writing was an help to the poet's judgment, by putting bounds to a wild overflowing fancy. I think, therefore, it will not be hard for me to make good what it was to prove. But you add, that were this let pass, yet he who wants judgment in the liberty of his fancy, may as well show the defect of it when he is confined to verse; for he who had judgment will avoid errors, and he who has it not, will commit them in all kinds of writing.

'This argument, as you have taken it from a most acute person, so I confess it carries much weight in it: but by using the word judgment here indefinitely, you seem to have put a fallacy upon us. I grant, he who has judgment, that is, so profound, so strong, so infallible a judgment, that he needs no helps to keep it always poised and upright, will commit no faults either in rhyme or out of it. And on the other extreme, he who has a judgment so weak and crazed that no helps can correct or amend it, shall write scurvily out of rhyme, and worse in it. But the first of these judgments is no where to be found, and the latter is not fit to write at all. To speak therefore of judgment as it is in the best poets; they who have the greatest proportion of it, want other helps than from it, within. As for example, you would be loth to say, that he who was endued with a sound judgment had no need of History, Geography, or Moral Philosophy, to write correctly. Judgment is indeed the master-workman in a play; but he requires many subordinate hands, many tools to his assistance. And verse I affirm to be one of these; 'tis a rule and line by which he keeps his building compact and even, which otherwise

lawless imagination would raise either irregularly or loosely.
At least, if the poet commits errors with this help, he would
make greater and more without it: 'tis, in short, a slow and
painful, but the surest kind of working. Ovid, whom you
accuse for luxuriancy in verse, had perhaps been farther guilty
of it, had he writ in prose. And for your instance of Ben
Johnson, who, you say, writ exactly without the help of rhyme;
you are to remember, 'tis only an aid to a luxuriant fancy,
which his was not: as he did not want imagination, so none
ever said he had much to spare. Neither was verse then refined
so much to be an help to that age, as it is to ours. Thus then
the second thoughts being usually the best, as receiving the
maturest digestion from judgment, and the last and most
mature product of those thoughts being artful and laboured
verse, it may well be inferred, that verse is a great help to a
luxuriant fancy; and this is what that argument which you
opposed was to evince.'

Neander was pursuing this discourse so eagerly, that Eugenius had called to him twice or thrice, ere he took notice
that the barge stood still, and that they were at the foot of
Somerset Stairs, where they had appointed it to land. The
company were all sorry to separate so soon, though a great
part of the evening was already spent; and stood a-while looking back on the water, which the moon-beams played upon,
and made it appear like floating quick-silver: at last they
went up through a crowd of French people, who were merrily
dancing in the open air, and nothing concerned for the noise
of guns which had alarmed the town that afternoon. Walking
thence together to the Piazze, they parted there; Eugenius and
Lisideius to some pleasant appointment they had made, and
Crites and Neander to their several lodgings.

A Defence of an Essay of Dramatic Poesy

Being an Answer to the Preface of 'The Great
Favourite, or, The Duke of Lerma'

[Prefixed to the Second Edition of *The Indian Emperor*, 1668]

THE FORMER edition of *The Indian Emperor* being full of faults, which had escaped the printer, I have been willing to overlook this second with more care; and though I could not allow myself so much time as was necessary, yet by that little I have done, the press is freed from some gross errors which it had to answer for before. As for the more material faults of writing, which are properly mine, though I see many of them, I want leisure to amend them. 'Tis enough for those who make one poem the business of their lives, to leave that correct: yet, excepting Virgil, I never met with any which was so in any language.

But while I was thus employed about this impression, there came to my hands a new printed play, called *The Great Favourite, or the Duke of Lerma;* the author [1] of which, a noble and most ingenious person, has done me the favour to make some observations and animadversions upon my Dramatic Essay. I must confess he might have better consulted his reputation, than by matching himself with so weak an adversary. But if his honour be diminished in the choice of his antagonist, it is sufficiently recompensed in the election of his cause: which being the weaker, in all appearance, as combating the received opinions of the best ancient and modern authors, will add to his glory, if he overcome, and to the opinion of his generosity, if he be vanquished, since he engages at so great odds, and, so like a cavalier, undertakes the protection of the

[1] Sir Robert Howard. See footnote 2 to *An Essay of Dramatic Poesy*.

weaker party. I have only to fear, on my own behalf, that so good a cause as mine may not suffer by my ill management, or weak defence; yet I cannot in honour but take the glove when 'tis offered me; though I am only a champion by succession, and no more able to defend the right of Aristotle and Horace, than an infant Dimock [2] to maintain the title of a king.

For my own concernment in the controversy, it is so small, that I can easily be contented to be driven from a few notions of Dramatic Poesy; especially by one, who has the reputation of understanding all things: and I might justly make that excuse for my yielding to him, which the philosopher made to the Emperor; why should I offer to contend with him, who is master of more than twenty legions of arts and sciences? But I am forced to fight, and therefore it will be no shame to be overcome.

Yet I am so much his servant, as not to meddle with anything which does not concern me in his Preface: therefore I leave the good sense and other excellencies of the first twenty lines, to be considered by the critics. As for the play of *The Duke of Lerma,* having so much altered and beautified it as he has done, it can justly belong to none but him. Indeed they must be extreme ignorant, as well as envious, who would rob him of that honour; for you see him putting in his claim to it, even in the first two lines:

> Repulse upon repulse, like waves thrown back,
> That slide to hang upon obdurate rocks.

After this, let detraction do its worst; for if this be not his, it deserves to be. For my part, I declare for distributive justice; and from this, and what follows, he certainly deserves *those advantages, which he acknowledges to have received from the opinion of sober men.*

In the next place, I must beg leave to observe his great address in courting the reader to his party. For, intending to

[2] The family of Dymokes were hereditary champions of England.

assault all poets, both ancient and modern, he discovers not his whole design at once, but seems only to aim at me, and attacks me on my weakest side, my defence of verse.

To begin with me, he gives me the compellation of 'The Author of *a Dramatic Essay*'; which is a little discourse in dialogue, for the most part borrowed from the observations of others; therefore, that I may not be wanting to him in civility, I return his compliment by calling him, 'The Author of *The Duke of Lerma.*'

But (that I may pass over his salute) he takes notice of my great pains to prove rhyme as natural in a serious play, and more effectual than blank verse. Thus indeed I did state the question; but he tells me, *I pursue that which I call natural in a wrong application; for 'tis not the question, whether rhyme, or not rhyme, be best, or most natural for a serious subject, but what is nearest the nature of that it represents.*

If I have formerly mistaken the question, I must confess my ignorance so far, as to say I continue still in my mistake: but he ought to have proved that I mistook it; for it is yet but *gratis dictum;* [3] I still shall think I have gained my point, if I can prove that rhyme is best, or most natural for a serious subject. As for the question as he states it, whether rhyme be nearest the nature of what it represents, I wonder he should think me so ridiculous as to dispute whether prose or verse be nearest to ordinary conversation.

It still remains for him to prove his inference; that, since verse is granted to be more remote than prose from ordinary conversation, therefore no serious plays ought to be writ in verse: and when he clearly makes that good, I will acknowledge his victory as absolute as he can desire it.

The question now is, which of us two has mistaken it; and if it appear I have not, the world will suspect, *what gentleman that was, who was allowed to speak twice in Parliament, because he had not yet spoken to the question;* and perhaps conclude it to be the same, who, as 'tis reported, maintained a

3 "Spoken gratuitously."

contradiction *in terminis,*[4] in the face of three hundred persons.[5]

But to return to verse; whether it be natural or not in plays, is a problem which is not demonstrable of either side: 'tis enough for me, that he acknowledges he had rather read good verse than prose: for if all the enemies of verse will confess as much, I shall not need to prove that it is natural. I am satisfied if it cause delight; for delight is the chief, if not the only, end of poesy: instruction can be admitted but in the second place, for poesy only instructs as it delights. 'Tis true, that to imitate well is a poet's work; but to affect the soul, and excite the passions, and, above all, to move admiration (which is the delight of serious plays), a bare imitation will not serve. The converse, therefore, which a poet is to imitate, must be heightened with all the arts and ornaments of poesy; and must be such as, strictly considered, could never be supposed spoken by any without premeditation.

As for what he urges, that *a play will still be supposed to be a composition of several persons speaking* ex tempore, *and that good verses are the hardest things which can be imagined to be so spoken;* I must crave leave to dissent from his opinion, as to the former part of it: for, if I am not deceived, a play is supposed to be the work of the poet, imitating or representing the conversation of several persons: and this I think to be as clear, as he thinks the contrary.

But I will be bolder, and do not doubt to make it good, though a paradox, that one great reason why prose is not to be used in serious plays, is, because it is too near the nature of converse: there may be too great a likeness; as the most skilful painters affirm, that there may be too near a resemblance in a picture: to take every lineament and feature is not to make an excellent piece, but to take so much only as will make a beautiful resemblance of the whole: and, with an ingenious flattery of nature, to heighten the beauties of some parts, and hide the deformities of the rest. For so says Horace,

---

[4] "Interminably."

[5] Sir Robert Howard, who was a member of Parliament.

> *Ut pictura poesis erit, etc. . . .*
> *Haec amat obscurum, vult haec sub luce videri,*
> *Judicis argutum quae non formidat acumen.*
>   *. . . Et quae*
> *Desperat tractata nitescere posse, relinquit.*[6]

In *Bartholomew Fair*, or the lowest kind of comedy, that degree of heightening is used, which is proper to set off that subject: it is true the author was not there to go out of prose, as he does in his higher arguments of Comedy, *The Fox* and *Alchymist;* yet he does so raise his matter in that prose, as to render it delightful; which he could never have performed, had he only said or done those very things, that are daily spoken or practised in the fair: for then the fair itself would be as full of pleasure to an ingenious person as the play, which we manifestly see it is not. But he hath made an excellent Lazar [7] of it; the copy is of price, though the original be vile. You see in *Catiline* and *Sejanus,* where the argument is great, he sometimes ascends to verse, which shows he thought it not unnatural in serious plays; and had his genius been as proper for rhyme as it was for humour, or had the age in which he lived attained to as much knowledge in verse as ours, it is probable he would have adorned those subjects with that kind of writing.

Thus Prose, though the rightful prince, yet is by common consent deposed, as too weak for the government of serious plays: and he failing, there now start up two competitors; one, the nearer in blood, which is Blank Verse; the other, more fit for the ends of government, which is Rhyme. Blank Verse is, indeed, the nearer Prose, but he is blemished with the weakness of his predecessor. Rhyme (for I will deal clearly) has somewhat of the usurper in him; but he is brave, and generous, and his dominion pleasing. For this reason of delight, the Ancients (whom I will still believe as wise as those who so

6 "Poetry is like painting. . . . This kind likes the shade, and that likes to be seen in the light and does not fear the sharp examination of critics. . . . And what he feels he cannot do well, he abandons" (*Art of Poetry* 361–364; 149–150).

7 Leper.

confidently correct them) wrote all their tragedies in verse,
though they knew it most remote from conversation.

But I perceive I am falling into the danger of another re-
buke from my opponent; for when I plead that the Ancients
used verse, I prove not they would have admitted rhyme, had
it then been written. All I can say is only this, that it seems to
have succeeded verse by the general consent of poets in all
modern languages; for almost all their serious plays are written in it; which, though it be no demonstration that therefore
they ought to be so, yet at least the practice first, and then the
continuation of it, shows that it attained the end, which was to
please; and if that cannot be compassed here, I will be the
first who shall lay it down. For I confess my chief endeavours
are to delight the age in which I live. If the humour of this
be for low comedy, small accidents, and raillery, I will force
my genius to obey it, though with more reputation I could
write in verse. I know I am not so fitted by nature to write
comedy: I want that gaiety of humour which is required to it.
My conversation is slow and dull; my humour saturnine and
reserved; in short, I am none of those who endeavour to break
jests in company, or make reparties. So that those, who decry
my comedies, do me no injury, except it be in point of profit:
reputation in them is the last thing to which I shall pretend.
I beg pardon for entertaining the reader with so ill a subject;
but before I quit that argument, which was the cause of this
digression, I cannot but take notice how I am corrected for
my quotation of Seneca, in my defence of plays in verse. My
words are these: 'Our language is noble, full, and significant;
and I know not why he, who is a master of it, may not clothe
ordinary things in it as decently as the Latin, if he use the
same diligence in his choice of words. One would think, *unlock a door,* was a thing as vulgar as could be spoken; yet
Seneca could be make it sound high and lofty in his Latin:

Reserate clusos regii postes laris.' [8]

But he says of me, 'That being filled with the precedents of

[8] See above, p. 70, footnote 96.

the Ancients, who writ their plays in verse, I commend the
thing, declaring our language to be full, noble, and significant, and charging all defects upon the *ill placing of words,*
which I prove by quoting Seneca loftily expressing such an
ordinary thing as *shutting a door.'*

Here he manifestly mistakes; for I spoke not of the placing,
but of the choice of words; for which I quoted that aphorism
of Julius Caesar, *Delectus verborum est origo eloquentiae;* [9]
but *delectus verborum* is no more Latin for the *placing of
words,* than *reserate* is Latin for *shut the door,* as he interprets
it, which I ignorantly construed *unlock* or *open* it.

He supposes I was highly affected with the sound of those
words, and I suppose I may more justly imagine it of him; for
if he had not been extremely satisfied with the sound, he
would have minded the sense a little better.

But these are now to be no faults; for ten days after his
book is published, and that his mistakes are grown so famous,
that they are come back to him, he sends his *Errata* to be
printed, and annexed to his play; and desired, that, instead of
shutting, you would read *opening,* which, it seems, was the
printer's fault. I wonder at his modesty, that he did nor rather
say it was Seneca's or mine; and that, in some authors *reserare*
was to *shut* as well as to *open,* as the word *barach,* say the
learned, is both to *bless* and *curse.*

Well, since it was the printer, he was a naughty man to
commit the same mistake twice in six lines: I warrant you
delectus verborum, for *placing of words,* was his mistake too,
though the author forgot to tell him of it: if it were my book,
I assure you I should. For those rascals ought to be the proxies
of every gentleman author, and to be chastised for him,
when he is not pleased to own an error. Yet since he has
given the *Errata,* I wish he would have enlarged them only
a few sheets more, and then he would have spared me the
labour of an answer: for this cursed printer is so given to mistakes, that there is scarce a sentence in the preface without
some false grammar, or hard sense in it; which will all be

9 See above, p. 70, footnote 95.

charged upon the poet, because he is so good-natured as to lay but three errors to the printer's account, and to take the rest upon himself, who is better able to support them. But he needs not apprehend that I should strictly examine those little faults, except I am called upon to do it: I shall return therefore to that quotation of Seneca, and answer, not to what he writes, but to what he means. I never intended it as an argument, but only as an illustration of what I had said before concerning the election of words; and all he can charge me with is only this, that if Seneca could make an ordinary thing sound well in Latin by the choice of words, the same, with the like care, might be performed in English: if it cannot, I have committed an error on the right hand, by commending too much the copiousness and well-sounding of our language, which I hope my countrymen will pardon me. At least the words which follow in my *Dramatic Essay* will plead somewhat in my behalf; for I say there, that this objection happens but seldom in a play; and then, too, either the meanness of the expression may be avoided, or shut out from the verse by breaking it in the midst.

But I have said too much in the defence of verse; for, after all, it is a very indifferent thing to me whether it obtain or not. I am content hereafter to be ordered by his rule, that is, to write it sometimes because it pleases me, and so much the rather, because he has declared that it pleases him. But he has taken his last farewell of the Muses, and he has done it civilly, by honouring them with the name of *his long acquaintances,* which is a compliment they have scarce deserved from him. For my own part, I bear a share in the public loss; and how emulous soever I may be of his fame and reputation, I cannot but give this testimony of his style, that it is extreme poetical, even in oratory; his thoughts elevated sometimes above common apprehension; his notions politic and grave, and tending to the instruction of Princes, and reformation of States; that they are abundantly interlaced with variety of fancies, tropes, and figures, which the critics have enviously branded with the name of obscurity and false grammar.

Well, he is now fettered in business of more unpleasant nature: the Muses have lost him, but the Commonwealth gains by it; the corruption of a poet is the generation of a statesman.

He will not venture again into the civil wars of censure, ubi—nullos habitura triumphos: [10] if he had not told us he had left the Muses, we might have half suspected it by that word *ubi*, which does not any way belong to them in that place: the rest of the verse is indeed Lucan's, but that *ubi*, I will answer for it, is his own. Yet he has another reason for this disgust of Poesy; for he says immediately after, that *the manner of plays which are now in most esteem is beyond his power to perform;* to perform the manner of a thing, I confess, is new English to me. *However, he condemns not the satisfaction of others, but rather their unnecessary understanding, who, like Sancho Pança's doctor, prescribe too strictly to our appetites; for,* says he, *in the difference of Tragedy and Comedy, and of Farce itself, there can be no determination but by the taste, nor in the manner of their composure.*

We shall see him now as great a critic as he was a poet; and the reason why he excelled so much in poetry will be evident, for it will appear to have proceeded from the exactness of his judgment. *In the difference of Tragedy, Comedy, and Farce itself, there can be no determination but by the taste.* I will not quarrel with the obscurity of his phrase, though I justly might; but beg his pardon if I do not rightly understand him. If he means that there is no essential difference betwixt Comedy, Tragedy, and Farce, but what is only made by the people's taste, which distinguishes one of them from the other, that is so manifest an error, that I need not lose time to contradict it. Were there neither judge, taste, nor opinion in the world, yet they would differ in their natures; for the action, character, and language of Tragedy, would still be great and high; that of Comedy, lower and more familiar; admiration would be the delight of one, and satire of the other.

[10] "Destined to have no victories" (Lucan, *Pharsalia* I. 12).

I have but briefly touched upon these things, because, whatever his words are, I can scarce imagine, that *he, who is always concerned for the true honour of reason, and would have no spurious issue fathered upon her,* should mean anything so absurd as to affirm, *that there is no difference betwixt Comedy and Tragedy but what is made by the taste only;* unless he would have us understand the comedies of my Lord L ——,[11] where the first act should be pottages, the second fricassees, &c., and the fifth a *chère entière* [12] of women.

I rather guess he means, that betwixt one comedy or tragedy and another, there is no other difference but what is made by the liking or disliking of the audience. This is indeed a less error than the former, but yet it is a great one. The liking or disliking of the people gives the play the denomination of good or bad, but does not really make or constitute it such. To please the people ought to be the poet's aim, because plays are made for their delight; but it does not follow that they are always pleased with good plays, or that the plays which please them are always good. The humour of the people is now for Comedy; therefore, in hope to please them, I write comedies rather than serious plays: and so far their taste prescribes to me: but it does not follow from that reason, that Comedy is to be preferred before Tragedy in its own nature; for that which is so in its own nature cannot be otherwise, as a man cannot but be a rational creature: but the opinion of the people may alter, and in another age, or perhaps in this, serious plays may be set up above comedies.

This I think a sufficient answer; if it be not, he has provided me of an excuse: it seems, in his wisdom, he foresaw my weakness, and has found out this expedient for me, *that it is not necessary for poets to study strict reason, since they are so used to a greater latitude than is allowed by that severe inquisition, that they must infringe their own jurisdiction, to profess themselves obliged to argue well.*

[11] Generally assumed to be John Maitland (1616–1682), second Earl and first Duke of Lauderdale.

[12] "Full feast."

I am obliged to him for discovering to me this back door; but I am not yet resolved on my retreat; for I am of opinion, that they cannot be good poets, who are not accustomed to argue well. False reasonings and colours of speech are the certain marks of one who does not understand the stage; for moral truth is the mistress of the poet as much as of the philosopher; Poesy must resemble natural truth, but it must *be* ethical. Indeed, the poet dresses truth, and adorns nature, but does not alter them:

Ficta voluptatis causa sint proxima veris.[13]

Therefore that is not the best poesy which resembles notions of things that are not, to things that are: though the fancy may be great and the words flowing, yet the soul is but half satisfied when there is not truth in the foundation. This is that which makes Virgil be preferred before the rest of poets. In variety of fancy, and sweetness of expression, you see Ovid far above him; for Virgil rejected many of those things which Ovid wrote. *A great wit's great work is to refuse,* as my worthy friend Sir John Berkenhead [14] has ingeniously expressed it: you rarely meet with anything in Virgil but truth, which therefore leaves the strongest impression of pleasure in the soul. This I thought myself obliged to say in behalf of Poesy; and to declare, though it be against myself, that when poets do not argue well, the defect is in the workmen, not in the art.

And now I come to the boldest part of his discourse, wherein he attacks not me, but all the Ancients and Moderns; and undermines, as he thinks, the very foundations on which Dramatic Poesy is built. I could wish he would have declined that envy which must of necessity follow such an undertaking, and contented himself with triumphing over me in my opinions of verse, which I will never hereafter dispute with him;

[13] "Let whatever is invented for the sake of pleasure be as near to the truth as possible" (*Art of Poetry* 338).

[14] John Berkenhead (1616–1679) was a critic and author of *Mercurius Aulicus*. The reference here is to his "In Memory of Mr. William Cartwright."

but he must pardon me if I have that veneration for Aristotle, Horace, Ben Johnson, and Corneille, that I dare not serve him in such a cause, and against such heroes, but rather fight under their protection, as Homer reports of little Teucer, who shot the Trojans from under the large buckler of Ajax Telamon:

Στῆ δ' ἄρ' ὑπ' Αἴαντος σάκεϊ Τελαμωνιάδαω, &c.

He stood beneath his brother's ample shield;
And cover'd there, shot death through all the field.[15]

The words of my noble adversary are these:

But if we examine the general rules laid down for plays by strict reason, we shall find the errors equally gross; for the great foundation which is laid to build upon, is nothing as it is generally stated, as will appear upon the examination of these particulars.

These particulars in due time shall be examined. In the meanwhile, let us consider what this great foundation is, which he says is nothing, as it is generally stated. I never heard of any other foundation of Dramatic Poesy than the imitation of Nature; neither was there ever pretended any other by the Ancients or Moderns, or me, who endeavour to follow them in that rule. This I have plainly said in my definition of a play; that it is a just and lively image of human nature, &c. Thus the foundation, as it is generally stated, will stand sure, if this definition of a play be true; if it be not, he ought to have made his exception against it, by proving that a play is not an imitation of Nature, but somewhat else, which he is pleased to think it.

But 'tis very plain, that he has mistaken the foundation for that which is built upon it, though not immediately: for the direct and immediate consequence is this; if Nature be to be imitated, then there is a rule for imitating Nature rightly; otherwise there may be an end, and no means conducing to it. Hitherto I have proceeded by demonstration; but as our divines, when they have proved a Deity, because there is order, and have inferred that this Deity ought to be worshipped,

15 *Iliad* VIII. 267.

differ afterwards in the manner of the worship; so, having laid down, that Nature is to be imitated, and that proposition proving the next, that then there are means which conduce to the imitating of Nature, I dare proceed no further positively; but have only laid down some opinions of the Ancients and Moderns, and of my own, as means which they used, and which I thought probable for the attaining of that end. Those means are the same which my antagonist calls the foundations, how properly the world may judge; and to prove that this is his meaning, he clears it immediately to you, by enumerating those rules or propositions against which he makes his particular exceptions; as, namely, those of Time and Place, in these words: *First, we are told the plot should not be so ridiculously contrived, as to crowd two several countries into one stage; secondly, to cramp the accidents of many years or days into the representation of two hours and a half; and, lastly, a conclusion drawn, that the only remaining dispute is, concerning time, whether it should be contained in twelve or twenty-four hours; and the place to be limited to that spot of ground where the play is supposed to begin: and this is called nearest Nature; for that is concluded most natural, which is most probable, and nearest to that which it presents.*

Thus he has only made a small mistake, of the means conducing to the end for the end itself, and of the superstructure for the foundation: but he proceeds: *to show therefore upon what ill grounds they dictate laws for Dramatic Poesy, &c.* He is here pleased to charge me with being magisterial, as he has done in many other places of his preface; therefore, in vindication of myself, I must crave leave to say, that my whole discourse was sceptical according to that way of reasoning which was used by Socrates, Plato, and all the Academics of old, which Tully and the best of the Ancients followed, and which is imitated by the modest inquisitions of the Royal Society. That it is so, not only the name will show, which is *an Essay*, but the frame and composition of the work. You see it is a dialogue sustained by persons of several opinions, all of them left doubtful, to be determined by the readers in general; and more particularly deferred to the accurate judgment of my Lord Buckhurst, to whom I made a dedication of my book. These are my words in my epistle, speaking of the persons whom I introduced in my dialogue: ' 'Tis true they differed in their opinions, as 'tis probable they would; neither do I take upon me to reconcile, but to relate them, leaving your Lordship to decide it in favour of that part which you shall judge most reasonable.' And after that, in my advertisement to the reader, I said this: 'The drift of the ensuing discourse is chiefly to vindicate the honour of our English writers from the censure of those who unjustly prefer the French before them. This I intimate, lest any should think me so exceeding vain, as to teach others an art, which they understand much better than myself.' But this is more than necessary to clear my modesty in that point: and I am very confident that there is scarce any man who has lost so much time, as to read that trifle, but will be my compurgator as to that arrogance whereof I am accused. The truth is, if I had been naturally guilty of so much vanity as to dictate my opinions; yet I do not find that the character of a positive or self-conceited person is of such advantage to any in this age, that I should labour to be publicly admitted of that order.

But I am not now to defend my own cause, when that of all the Ancients and Moderns is in question: for this gentleman, who accuses me of arrogance, has taken a course not to be taxed with the other extreme of modesty. Those propositions which are laid down in my discourse as helps to the better imitation of Nature, are not mine (as I have said), nor were ever pretended so to be, but derived from the authority of Aristotle and Horace, and from the rules and examples of Ben Johnson and Corneille. These are the men with whom properly he contends, and against *whom he will endeavour to make it evident, that there is no such thing as what they all pretend.*

His argument against the Unities of Place and Time is this: *that 'tis as impossible for one stage to present two rooms or houses truly, as two countries or kingdoms; and as impossible that five hours or twenty-four hours should be two hours, as*

that a thousand hours or years should be less than what they
are, or the greatest part of time to be comprehended in the
less: for all of them being impossible, they are none of them
nearest the truth, or nature of what they present; for impossi-
bilities are all equal, and admit of no degree.

This argument is so scattered into parts, that it can scarce
be united into a syllogism; yet, in obedience to him, *I will ab-*
breviate, and comprehend as much of it as I can in few words,
that my answer to it may be more perspicuous. I conceive his
meaning to be what follows, as to the Unity of Place: (if I
mistake, I beg his pardon, professing it is not out of any design to play the *Argumentative Poet*). If one stage cannot
properly present two rooms or houses, much less two countries or kingdoms, then there can be no Unity of Place. But
one stage cannot properly perform this: therefore there can be
no Unity of Place.

I plainly deny his minor proposition; the force of which, if
I mistake not, depends on this, that the stage being one place
cannot be two. This indeed is as great a secret, as that we are
all mortal; but to requite it with another, I must crave leave
to tell him, that though the stage cannot be two places, yet it
may properly represent them successively, or at several times.
His argument is indeed no more than a mere fallacy, which
will evidently appear when we distinguish place, as it relates
to plays, into real and imaginary. The real place is that
theatre, or piece of ground, on which the play is acted. The
imaginary, that house, town, or country where the action of
the drama is supposed to be, or, more plainly, where the scene
of the play is laid. Let us now apply this to that Herculean
argument, *which if strictly and duly weighed, is to make it*
evident that there is no such thing as what they all pretend.
'Tis impossible, he says, for one stage to present two rooms
or houses: I answer, 'tis neither impossible, nor improper, for
one real place to represent two or more imaginary places, so
it be done successively; which in other words, is no more than
this, that the imagination of the audience, aided by the words
of the poet, and painted scenes, may suppose the stage to be

sometimes one place, sometimes another; now a garden, or wood, and immediately a camp: which I appeal to every man's imagination, if it be not true. Neither the Ancients nor Moderns, as much fools as he is pleased to think them, ever asserted that they could make one place two; but they might hope, by the good leave of this author, that the change of a scene might lead the imagination to suppose the place altered: so that he cannot fasten those absurdities upon this scene of a play, or imaginary place of action, that it is one place, and yet two. And this being so clearly proved, that 'tis past any show of a reasonable denial, it will not be hard to destroy that other part of his argument, which depends upon it, namely, that 'tis as impossible for a stage to represent two rooms or houses, as two countries or kingdoms: for this reason is already overthrown, which was, because both were alike impossible. This is manifestly otherwise; for 'tis proved that a stage may properly represent two rooms or houses; for the imagination being judge of what is represented, will in reason be less shocked with the appearance of two rooms in the same house, or two houses in the same city, than with two distant cities in the same country, or two remote countries in the same universe. Imagination in a man, or reasonable creature, is supposed to participate of Reason, and when that governs, as it does in the belief of fiction, Reason is not destroyed, but misled, or blinded; that can prescribe to the Reason, during the time of the representation, somewhat like a weak belief of what it sees and hears; and Reason suffers itself to be so hoodwinked, that it may better enjoy the pleasures of the fiction: but it is never so wholly made a captive, as to be drawn headlong into a persuasion of those things which are most remote from probability: 'tis in that case a free-born subject, not a slave; it will contribute willingly its assent, as far as it sees convenient, but will not be forced. Now, there is a greater vicinity in nature betwixt two rooms than betwixt two houses; betwixt two houses, than betwixt two cities; and so of the rest: Reason, therefore, can sooner be led by imagination to step from one room to another, than to walk to two distant houses, and yet rather to go thither, than to fly like a witch through the air, and be hurried from one region to another. Fancy and Reason go hand in hand; the first cannot leave the last behind: and though Fancy, when it sees the wide gulf, would venture over, as the nimbler, yet it is withheld by Reason, which will refuse to take the leap, when the distance over it appears too large. If Ben Johnson himself will remove the scene from Rome into Tuscany in the same act, and from thence return to Rome, in the scene which immediately follows, Reason will consider there is no proportionable allowance of time to perform the journey, and, therefore, will choose to stay at home. So, then, the less change of place there is, the less time is taken up in transporting the persons of the drama, with analogy to reason; and in that analogy, or resemblance of fiction to truth, consists the excellency of the play.

For what else concerns the Unity of Place, I have already given my opinion of it in my *Essay,* that there is a latitude to be allowed to it, as several places in the same town or city, or places adjacent to each other in the same country; which may all be comprehended under the larger denomination of one place; yet with this restriction, that the nearer and fewer those imaginary places are, the greater resemblance they will have to truth; and reason, which cannot make them one, will be more easily led to suppose them so.

What has been said of the Unity of Place, may easily be applied to that of Time: I grant it to be impossible, that the greater part of time should be comprehended in the less, that twenty-four hours should be crowded into three: but there is no necessity of that supposition; for as *place,* so *time* relating to a play, is either imaginary or real: the real is comprehended in those three hours, more or less, in the space of which the play is represented; the imaginary is that which is supposed to be taken up in the representation, as twenty-four hours, more or less. Now, no man ever could suppose, that twenty-four real hours could be included in the space of three; but where is the absurdity of affirming, that the feigned business of twenty-four imagined hours, may not more naturally be represented in the compass of three real hours, than the like feigned business of twenty-four years in the same proportion of real time? For the proportions are always real, and much nearer, by his permission, of twenty-four to three, than of four thousand to it.

I am almost fearful of illustrating anything by similitude, lest he should confute it for an argument; yet I think the comparison of a glass will discover very aptly the fallacy of his argument, both concerning time and place. The strength of his reason depends on this, that the less cannot comprehend the greater. I have already answered, that we need not suppose it does; I say not that the less can comprehend the greater, but only, that it may represent it; as in a glass, or mirror, of half-a-yard diameter, a whole room, and many persons in it, may be seen at once; not that it can comprehend that room, or those persons, but that it represents them to the sight.

But the author of the *Duke of Lerma* is to be excused for his declaring against the Unity of Time; for, if I be not much mistaken, he is an interested person—the time of that play taking up so many years as the favour of the Duke of Lerma continued; nay, the second and third act including all the time of his prosperity, which was a great part of the reign of Philip the Third: for in the beginning of the second act he was not yet a favourite, and before the end of the third, was in disgrace. I say not this with the least design of limiting the stage too servilely to twenty-four hours, however he be pleased to tax me with dogmatising on that point. In my Dialogue, as I before hinted, several persons maintained their several opinions: one of them, indeed, who supported the cause of the French Poesy, said how strict they were in that particular; but he who answered, in behalf of our nation, was willing to give more latitude to the rule, and cites the words of Corneille himself, complaining against the severity of it, and observing, what beauties it banished from the stage, *pag.* 44 [16] of my

[16] In the original edition and, coincidentally, p. 44, above.

Essay. In few words, my own opinion is this (and I willingly submit it to my adversary, when he will please impartially to consider it) that the imaginary time of every play ought to be contrived into as narrow a compass, as the nature of the plot, the quality of persons, and variety of accidents will allow. In Comedy, I would not exceed twenty-four or thirty hours; for the plot, accidents, and persons, of Comedy are small, and may be naturally turned in a little compass: but in Tragedy, the design is weighty, and the persons great; therefore, there will naturally be required a greater space of time in which to move them. And this, though Ben Johnson has not told us, yet it is manifestly his opinion: for you see that to his comedies he allows generally but twenty-four hours; to his two tragedies, *Sejanus* and *Catiline,* a much larger time, though he draws both of them into as narrow a compass as he can: for he shows you only the latter end of Sejanus his favour, and the conspiracy of Catiline already ripe, and just breaking out into action.

But as it is an error, on the one side, to make too great a disproportion betwixt the imaginary time of the play, and the real time of its representation; so, on the other side, 'tis an oversight to compress the accidents of a play into a narrower compass than that in which they could naturally be produced. Of this last error the French are seldom guilty, because the thinness of their plots prevents them from it; but few Englishmen, except Ben Johnson, have ever made a plot, with variety of design in it, included in twenty-four hours, which was altogether natural. For this reason, I prefer the *Silent Woman* before all other plays, I think justly, as I do its author, in judgment, above all other poets. Yet, of the two, I think that error the most pardonable which in too strait a compass crowds together many accidents, since it produces more variety, and, consequently, more pleasure to the audience; and because the nearness of proportion betwixt the imaginary and real time, does speciously cover the compression of the accidents.

Thus I have endeavoured to answer the meaning of his

argument; for, as he drew it, I humbly conceive that it was none—as will appear by his proposition, and the proof of it. His proposition was this:

If strictly and duly weighed, it is as impossible for one stage to present two rooms, or houses, as two countries, or kingdoms, &c. And his proof this: *For all being impossible, they are none of them nearest the truth or nature of what they present.*

Here you see, instead of proof, or reason, there is only *petitio principii.*[17] For, in plain words, his sense is this: two things are as impossible as one another, because they are both equally impossible: but he takes those two things to be granted as impossible, which he ought to have proved such before he had proceeded to prove them equally impossible: he should have made out first, that it was impossible for one stage to represent two houses, and then have gone forward to prove, that it was equally impossible for a stage to present two houses, as two countries.

After all this, the very absurdity, to which he would reduce me, is none at all: for he only drives at this, that, if his argument be true, I must then acknowledge that there are degrees in impossibilities, which I easily grant him without dispute; and, if I mistake not, Aristotle and the School are of my opinion. For there are some things which are absolutely impossible, and others which are only so *ex parte;* [18] as it is absolutely impossible for a thing *to be,* and *not to be* at the same time: but for a stone to move naturally upward, is only impossible *ex parte materiae;* [19] but it is not impossible for the First Mover to alter the nature of it.

His last assault, like that of a Frenchman, is most feeble; for whereas I have observed, that none have been violent against verse, but such only as have not attempted it, or have succeeded ill in their attempt, he will needs, according to his usual custom, improve my observation to an argument, that he might have the glory to confute it. But I lay my observation

17 "Begging the question."
18 "From nature."
19 "From the nature of the material."

at his feet, as I do my pen, which I have often employed willingly in his deserved commendations, and now most unwill-
ingly against his judgment. For his person and parts, I honour
them as much as any man living, and have had so many particular obligations to him, that I should be very ungrateful, if
I did not acknowledge them to the world. But I gave not
the first occasion of this difference in opinions. In my epistle
dedicatory, before my *Rival Ladies,* I had said somewhat in
behalf of verse, which he was pleased to answer in his preface
to his plays: that occasioned my reply in my *Essay;* and that
reply begot this rejoinder of his, in his preface to the *Duke of
Lerma.* But as I was the last who took up arms, I will be the
first to lay them down. For what I have here written, I submit
it wholly to him; and if I do not hereafter answer what may
be objected against this paper, I hope the world will not im-
pute it to any other reason, than only the due respect which
I have for so noble an opponent.

Preface to the Fables

[1700]

'TIS WITH a Poet, as with a man who designs to build, and is very exact, as he supposes, in casting up the cost beforehand; but, generally speaking, he is mistaken in his account, and reckons short of the expense he first intended. He alters his mind as the work proceeds, and will have this or that convenience more, of which he had not thought when he began. So has it happened to me; I have built a house, where I intended but a lodge; yet with better success than a certain nobleman,[1] who, beginning with a dog-kennel, never lived to finish the palace he had contrived.

From translating the First of Homer's *Iliads*, (which I intended as an essay to the whole work) I proceeded to the translation of the Twelfth Book of Ovid's *Metamorphoses*, because it contains, among other things, the causes, the beginning, and ending of the Trojan war. Here I ought in reason to have stopped; but the speeches of Ajax and Ulysses lying next in my way, I could not balk 'em. When I had compassed them, I was so taken with the former part of the Fifteenth Book (which is the masterpiece of the whole *Metamorphoses*) that I enjoined myself the pleasing task of rendering it into English. And now I found, by the number of my verses, that they began to swell into a little volume; which gave me an occasion of looking backward on some beauties of my author, in his former books: there occurred to me the *Hunting of the Boar, Cinyras and Myrrha,* the good-natured story of *Baucis and Philemon,* with the rest, which I hope I have translated closely enough, and given them the same turn of verse which they had in the original; and this, I may say, without vanity, is not the talent of every poet. He who

[1] George Villiers, second Duke of Buckingham.

94

has arrived the nearest to it, is the ingenious and learned Sandys,[2] the best versifier of the former age; if I may properly call it by that name, which was the former part of this concluding century. For Spenser and Fairfax both flourished in the reign of Queen Elizabeth; great masters in our language, and who saw much farther into the beauties of our numbers than those who immediately followed them. Milton was the poetical son of Spenser, and Mr. Waller of Fairfax; for we have our lineal descents and clans as well as other families. Spenser more than once insinuates, that the soul of Chaucer was transfused into his body; and that he was begotten by him two hundred years after his decease. Milton has acknowledged to me, that Spenser was his original; and many besides myself have heard our famous Waller own, that he derived the harmony of his numbers from *Godfrey of Bulloign,* which was turned into English by Mr. Fairfax.[3]

But to return: having done with Ovid for this time, it came into my mind, that our old English poet, Chaucer, in many things resembled him, and that with no disadvantage on the side of the modern author, as I shall endeavour to prove when I compare them; and as I am, and always have been, studious to promote the honour of my native country, so I soon resolved to put their merits to the trial, by turning some of the *Canterbury Tales* into our language, as it is now refined; for by this means both the poets being set in the same light, and dressed in the same English habit, story to be compared with story, a certain judgment may be made betwixt them by the reader, without obtruding my opinion on him. Or if I seem partial to my countryman, and predecessor in the laurel, the friends of antiquity are not few; and, besides many of the learned, Ovid has almost all the *Beaux,* and the whole Fair Sex, his declared patrons. Perhaps I have assumed somewhat more to myself than they allow me, because I have adventured to sum up the evidence; but the readers are the jury, and

---

2 See above, footnote 87, p. 65.

3 Edward Fairfax (d. 1635). *Godfrey of Bulloigne, or the Recovery of Jerusalem* was his translation of Tasso's *Gerusalemme liberata.*

their privilege remains entire, to decide according to the
merits of the cause; or, if they please, to bring it to another
hearing before some other court. In the mean time, to follow
the thrid of my discourse (as thoughts, according to Mr.
Hobbes,[4] have always some connexion) so from Chaucer I
was led to think on Boccace, who was not only his contemporary, but also pursued the same studies; wrote novels in prose,
and many works in verse; particularly is said to have invented
the octave rhyme, or stanza of eight lines, which ever since has
been maintained by the practice of all Italian writers who are,
or at least assume the title of heroic poets. He and Chaucer,
among other things, had this in common, that they refined
their mother-tongues; but with this difference, that Dante had
begun to file their language, at least in verse, before the time
of Boccace, who likewise received no little help from his master Petrarch; but the reformation of their prose was wholly
owing to Boccace himself, who is yet the standard of purity
in the Italian tongue, though many of his phrases are become
obsolete, as in process of time it must needs happen. Chaucer
(as you have formerly been told by our learned Mr. Rymer)[5]
first adorned and amplified our barren tongue from the
Provençal, which was then the most polished of all the modern
languages; but this subject has been copiously treated by that
great critic, who deserves no little commendation from us his
countrymen. For these reasons of time, and resemblance of
genius, in Chaucer and Boccace, I resolved to join them in my
present work; to which I have added some original papers
of my own, which whether they are equal or inferior to my
other poems, an author is the most improper judge; and therefore I leave them wholly to the mercy of the reader. I will
hope the best, that they will not be condemned; but if they
should, I have the excuse of an old gentleman, who, mount-
ing on horseback before some ladies, when I was present, got
up somewhat heavily, but desired of the fair spectators, that

4 Thomas Hobbes (1588–1679), the English philosopher.
5 Thomas Rymer (1641–1713), critic and historian, author of *A Short
View of Tragedy* (1693).

they would count fourscore and eight before they judged him. By the mercy of God, I am already come within twenty years of his number, a cripple in my limbs, but what decays are in my mind, the reader must determine. I think myself as vigorous as ever in the faculties of my soul, excepting only my memory, which is not impaired to any great degree; and if I lose not more of it, I have no great reason to complain. What judgment I had, increases rather than diminishes; and thoughts, such as they are, come crowding in so fast upon me, that my only difficulty is to choose or to reject, to run them into verse, or to give them the other harmony of prose: I have so long studied and practised both, that they are grown into a habit, and become familiar to me. In short, though I may lawfully plead some part of the old gentleman's excuse, yet I will reserve it till I think I have greater need, and ask no grains of allowance for the faults of this my present work, but those which are given of course to human frailty. I will not trouble my reader with the shortness of time in which I writ it, or the several intervals of sickness. They who think too well of their own performances, are apt to boast in their prefaces how little time their works have cost them, and what other business of more importance interfered; but the reader will be as apt to ask the question, why they allowed not a longer time to make their works more perfect? and why they had so despicable an opinion of their judges as to thrust their indigested stuff upon them, as if they deserved no better?

With this account of my present undertaking, I conclude the first part of this discourse: in the second part, as at a second sitting, though I alter not the draught, I must touch the same features over again, and change the dead-colouring [6] of the whole. In general I will only say, that I have written nothing which savours of immorality or profaneness; at least, I am not conscious to myself of any such intention. If there happen to be found an irreverent expression, or a thought too wanton, they are crept into my verses through my inadvertency: if the searchers find any in the cargo, let them be staved

[6] A first layer of paint.

or forfeited, like counterbanded goods; at least, let their authors be answerable for them, as being but imported merchandise, and not of my own manufacture. On the other side, I have endeavoured to choose such fables, both ancient and modern, as contain in each of them some instructive moral, which I could prove by induction, but the way is tedious; and they leap foremost into sight, without the reader's trouble of looking after them. I wish I could affirm with a safe conscience, that I had taken the same care in all my former writings; for it must be owned, that supposing verses are never so beautiful or pleasing, yet, if they contain anything which shocks religion or good manners, they are at best what Horace says of good numbers without good sense, *Versus inopes rerum nugaeque canorae.*[7] Thus far, I hope, I am right in court, without renouncing to my other right of self-defence, where I have been wrongfully accused, and my sense wire-drawn into blasphemy or bawdry, as it has often been by a religious lawyer, in a late pleading against the stage;[8] in which he mixes truth with falsehood, and has not forgotten the old rule of calumniating strongly, that something may remain.

I resume the thrid of my discourse with the first of my translations, which was the first *Iliad* of Homer. If it shall please God to give me longer life, and moderate health, my intentions are to translate the whole *Ilias;* provided still that I meet with those encouragements from the public, which may enable me to proceed in my undertaking with some cheerfulness. And this I dare assure the world beforehand, that I have found, by trial, Homer a more pleasing task than Virgil, though I say not the translation will be less laborious; for the Grecian is more according to my genius than the Latin poet. In the works of the two authors we may read their manners, and natural inclinations, which are wholly different. Virgil was of a quiet, sedate temper; Homer was violent, impetuous, and full of fire. The chief talent of Virgil was propriety of thoughts, and

[7] "Verses without matter and trivial songs" (*Art of Poetry* 322).

[8] The reference is to Jeremy Collier (1650–1726) and to his famous *A Short View of the Immorality and Profaneness of the English Stage* (1698).

ornament of words: Homer was rapid in his thoughts, and took all the liberties, both of numbers and of expressions, which his language, and the age in which he lived, allowed him. Homer's invention was more copious, Virgil's more confined; so that if Homer had not led the way, it was not in Virgil to have begun heroic poetry; for nothing can be more evident, than that the Roman poem is but the second part of the *Ilias;* a continuation of the same story, and the persons already formed. The manners of Aeneas are those of Hector, superadded to those which Homer gave him. The adventures of Ulysses in the *Odysseis* are imitated in the first Six Books of Virgil's *Aeneis;* and though the accidents are not the same (which would have argued him of a servile copying, and total barrenness of invention), yet the seas were the same in which both the heroes wandered; and Dido cannot be denied to be the poetical daughter of Calypso. The six latter Books of Virgil's poem are the four-and-twenty *Iliads* contracted; a quarrel occasioned by a lady, a single combat, battles fought, and a town besieged. I say not this in derogation to Virgil, neither do I contradict anything which I have formerly said in his just praise; for his episodes are almost wholly of his own invention, and the form which he has given to the telling makes the tale his own, even though the original story had been the same. But this proves, however, that Homer taught Virgil to design; and if invention be the first virtue of an epic poet, then the Latin poem can only be allowed the second place. Mr. Hobbes, in the preface to his own bald translation of the *Ilias* (studying poetry as he did mathematics, when it was too late), Mr. Hobbes, I say, begins the praise of Homer where he should have ended it. He tells us, that the first beauty of an epic poem consists in diction; that is, in the choice of words, and harmony of numbers. Now the words are the colouring of the work, which, in the order of nature, is last to be considered. The design, the disposition, the manners, and the thoughts, are all before it: where any of those are wanting or imperfect, so much wants or is imperfect in the imitation of human life, which is in the very definition of a poem. Words, indeed, like glaring colours, are the first beauties that arise and strike the sight; but, if the draught be false or lame, the figures ill disposed, the manners obscure or inconsistent, or the thoughts unnatural, then the finest colours are but daubing, and the piece is a beautiful monster at the best. Neither Virgil nor Homer were deficient in any of the former beauties; but in this last, which is expression, the Roman poet is at least equal to the Grecian, as I have said elsewhere: supplying the poverty of his language by his musical ear, and by his diligence.

But to return: our two great poets being so different in their tempers, one choleric and sanguine, the other phlegmatic and melancholic; that which makes them excel in their several ways is, that each of them has followed his own natural inclination, as well in forming the design, as in the execution of it. The very heroes show their authors: Achilles is hot, impatient, revengeful—

> *Impiger, iracundus, inexorabilis, acer, &c.*,[9]

Aeneas patient, considerate, careful of his people, and merciful to his enemies; ever submissive to the will of heaven—

> *quo fata trahunt retrahuntque, sequamur.*[10]

I could please myself with enlarging on this subject, but am forced to defer it to a fitter time. From all I have said, I will only draw this inference, that the action of Homer, being more full of vigour than that of Virgil, according to the temper of the writer, is of consequence more pleasing to the reader. One warms you by degrees; the other sets you on fire all at once, and never intermits his heat. 'Tis the same difference which Longinus makes betwixt the effects of eloquence in Demosthenes and Tully; one persuades, the other commands. You never cool while you read Homer, even not in the Second Book (a graceful flattery to his countrymen); but he hastens from the ships, and concludes not that book till he has made

[9] "Active, wrathful, implacable, and fierce" (Horace, *Art of Poetry* 121).
[10] "Wherever the fates lead, let us follow" (Virgil, *Aeneid* V. 709).

you an amends by the violent playing of a new machine. From thence he hurries on his action with variety of events, and ends it in less compass than two months. This vehemence of his, I confess, is more suitable to my temper; and therefore I have translated his First Book with greater pleasure than any part of Virgil; but it was not a pleasure without pains. The continual agitations of the spirits must needs be a weakening of any constitution, especially in age; and many pauses are required for refreshment betwixt the heats; the *Iliad* of itself being a third part longer than all Virgil's works together.

This is what I thought needful in this place to say of Homer. I proceed to Ovid and Chaucer; considering the former only in relation to the latter. With Ovid ended the golden age of the Roman tongue; from Chaucer the purity of the English tongue began. The manners of the poets were not unlike. Both of them were well-bred, well-natured, amorous, and libertine, at least in their writings, it may be also in their lives. Their studies were the same, philosophy and philology. Both of them were knowing in astronomy; of which Ovid's books of the Roman Feasts, and Chaucer's Treatise of the Astrolabe, are sufficient witnesses. But Chaucer was likewise an astrologer, as were Virgil, Horace, Persius, and Manilius. Both writ with wonderful facility and clearness; neither were great inventors: for Ovid only copied the Grecian fables, and most of Chaucer's stories were taken from his Italian contemporaries, or their predecessors. Boccace his *Decameron* was first published, and from thence our Englishman has borrowed many of his *Canterbury Tales:* yet that of Palamon and Arcite was written, in all probability, by some Italian wit, in a former age, as I shall prove hereafter. The tale of Grizild [11] was the invention of Petrarch; by him sent to Boccace, from whom it came to Chaucer. *Troilus and Cressida* [12] was also written by a Lombard author, but much amplified by our English translator,

[11] "Palamon and Arcite" is Chaucer's "Knight's Tale"; "the tale of Grizild" is the "Clerk's Tale."

[12] The main source of Chaucer's *Troilus and Cressida* was Boccaccio's *Il Filostrato.*

as well as beautified; the genius of our countrymen in general being rather to improve an invention than to invent themselves, as is evident not only in our poetry, but in many of our manufactures. I find I have anticipated already, and taken up from Boccace before I come to him: but there is so much less behind; and I am of the temper of most kings, who love to be in debt, are all for present money, no matter how they pay it afterwards: besides, the nature of a preface is rambling, never wholly out of the way, nor in it. This I have learned from the practice of honest Montaigne, and return at my pleasure to Ovid and Chaucer, of whom I have little more to say.

Both of them built on the inventions of other men; yet since Chaucer had something of his own, as the Wife of Bath's Tale, the *Cock and the Fox*,[13] which I have translated, and some others, I may justly give our countryman the precedence in that part; since I can remember nothing of Ovid which was wholly his. Both of them understood the manners; under which name I comprehend the passions, and, in a larger sense, the descriptions of persons, and their very habits. For an example, I see Baucis and Philemon as perfectly before me, as if some ancient painter had drawn them; and all the Pilgrims in the *Canterbury Tales,* their humours, their features, and the very dress, as distinctly as if I had supped with them at the Tabard in Southwark. Yet even there too the figures of Chaucer are much more lively, and set in a better light; which though I have not time to prove, yet I appeal to the reader, and am sure he will clear me from partiality. The thoughts and words remain to be considered, in the comparison of the two poets, and I have saved myself one-half of the labour, by owning that Ovid lived when the Roman tongue was in its meridian; Chaucer, in the dawning of our language: therefore that part of the comparison stands not on an equal foot, any more than the diction of Ennius and Ovid, or of Chaucer and our present English. The words are given up as a post not to be defended in our poet, because he wanted the modern art

13 "The Cock and the Fox" is the "Nun's Priest's Tale."

of fortifying. The thoughts remain to be considered: and they
are to be measured only by their propriety; that is, as they
flow more or less naturally from the persons described, on such
and such occasions. The vulgar judges, which are nine parts
in ten of all nations, who call conceits and jingles wit, who see
Ovid full of them, and Chaucer altogether without them, will
think me little less than mad for preferring the Englishman
to the Roman. Yet, with their leave, I must presume to say,
that the things they admire are only glittering trifles, and so
far from being witty, that in a serious poem they are nauseous,
because they are unnatural. Would any man who is ready to
die for love, describe his passion like Narcissus? Would he
think of *inopem me copia fecit*,[14] and a dozen more of such
expressions, poured on the neck of one another, and signifying
all the same thing? If this were wit, was this a time to be
witty, when the poor wretch was in the agony of death? This
is just John Littlewit in *Bartholomew Fair*, who had a conceit (as he tells you) left him in his misery; a miserable conceit.
On these occasions the poet should endeavour to raise pity;
but, instead of this, Ovid is tickling you to laugh. Virgil never
made use of such machines when he was moving you to com-
miserate the death of Dido: he would not destroy what he was
building. Chaucer makes Arcite violent in his love, and un-
just in the pursuit of it; yet, when he came to die, he made
him think more reasonably: he repents not of his love, for
that had altered his character; but acknowledges the injustice
of his proceedings, and resigns Emilia to Palamon. What
would Ovid have done on this occasion? He would certainly
have made Arcite witty on his deathbed; he had complained
he was further off from possession, by being so near, and a
thousand such boyisms, which Chaucer rejected as below the
dignity of the subject. They who think otherwise, would, by
the same reason, prefer Lucan and Ovid to Homer and Virgil, and Martial to all four of them. As for the turn of words,
in which Ovid particularly excels all poets, they are sometimes a fault, and sometimes a beauty, as they are used prop-

[14] "Abundance has made me poor" (Ovid, *Metamorphoses* III. 466).

erly or improperly; but in strong passions always to be
shunned, because passions are serious, and will admit no playing. The French have a high value for them; and, I confess,
they are often what they call delicate, when they are introduced with judgment; but Chaucer writ with more simplicity,
and followed Nature more closely, than to use them. I have
thus far, to the best of my knowledge, been an upright judge
betwixt the parties in competition, not meddling with the design nor the disposition of it; because the design was not their
own; and in the disposing of it they were equal. It remains
that I say somewhat of Chaucer in particular.

In the first place, as he is the father of English poetry, so I
hold him in the same degree of veneration as the Grecians
held Homer, or the Romans Virgil. He is a perpetual fountain
of good sense; learn'd in all sciences; and, therefore, speaks
properly on all subjects. As he knew what to say, so he knows
also when to leave off; a continence which is practised by few
writers, and scarcely by any of the ancients, excepting Virgil
and Horace. One of our late great poets [15] is sunk in his reputation, because he could never forgive any conceit which came
in his way; but swept like a drag-net, great and small. There
was plenty enough, but the dishes were ill sorted; whole pyr-
amids of sweetmeats, for boys and women; but little of solid
meat, for men. All this proceeded not from any want of knowledge, but of judgment. Neither did he want that in discerning
the beauties and faults of other poets, but only indulged himself in the luxury of writing; and perhaps knew it was a fault,
but hoped the reader would not find it. For this reason, though
he must always be thought a great poet, he is no longer esteemed a good writer; and for ten impressions, which his works
have had in so many successive years, yet at present a hundred
books are scarcely purchased once a twelvemonth; for, as my
last Lord Rochester said, though somewhat profanely, *Not
being of God, he could not stand.*

Chaucer followed Nature everywhere, but was never so bold
to go beyond her; and there is a great difference of being

15 Abraham Cowley (1618–1667).

poeta and *nimis poeta*,[16] if we may believe Catullus, as much as betwixt a modest behaviour and affectation. The verse of Chaucer, I confess, is not harmonious to us; but 'tis like the eloquence of one whom Tacitus commends, it was *auribus istius temporis accommodata:* [17] they who lived with him, and some time after him, thought it musical; and it continues so even in our judgment, if compared with the numbers of Lidgate and Gower, his contemporaries: there is the rude sweetness of a Scotch tune in it, which is natural and pleasing, though not perfect. 'Tis true, I cannot go so far as he who published the last edition [18] of him; for he would make us believe the fault is in our ears, and that there were really ten syllables in a verse where we find but nine: but this opinion is not worth confuting; [19] 'tis so gross and obvious an error, that common sense (which is a rule in everything but matters of Faith and Revelation) must convince the reader that equality of numbers, in every verse which we call *heroic,* was either not known, or not always practised, in Chaucer's age. It were an easy matter to produce some thousands of his verses, which are lame for want of half a foot, and sometimes a whole one, and which no pronunciation can make otherwise. We can only say, that he lived in the infancy of our poetry, and that nothing is brought to perfection at the first. We must be children before we grow men. There was an Ennius, and in the process of time a Lucilius, and a Lucretius, before Virgil and Horace; even after Chaucer there was a Spenser, a Harrington,[20] a Fairfax, before Waller and Denham were in being; and our numbers were in their nonage till these last appeared. I need say little of his parentage, life, and fortunes; they are

[16] "Too much a poet" (Martial, *Epigrams* III. 44. 4). Dryden errs in attributing to Catullus a quotation from Martial.

[17] "Suited to the ears of that time" (*Dialogue on Orators* 21).

[18] Thomas Speght's edition of Chaucer was published in 1597 and 1602.

[19] Dryden is of course in error, but it should be noted that the basic principles of Chaucer's versification were not elucidated until 1775.

[20] Sir John Harington (1561–1612), English author who translated *Orlando Furioso.*

to be found at large in all the editions of his works. He was employed abroad, and favoured, by Edward the Third, Richard the Second, and Henry the Fourth, and was poet, as I suppose, to all three of them. In Richard's time, I doubt, he was a little dipt in the rebellion of the Commons; and being brother-in-law to John of Ghant, it was no wonder if he followed the fortunes of that family; and was well with Henry the Fourth when he had deposed his predecessor. Neither is it to be admired, that Henry, who was a wise as well as a valiant prince, who claimed by succession, and was sensible that his title was not sound, but was rightfully in Mortimer, who had married the heir of York; it was not to be admired, I say, if the great politician should be pleased to have the greatest Wit of those times in his interests, and to be the trumpet of his praises. Augustus had given him the example, by the advice of Maecenas, who recommended Virgil and Horace to him; whose praises helped to make him popular while he was alive, and after his death have made him precious to posterity. As for the religion of our poet, he seems to have some little bias towards the opinion of Wickliff, after John of Ghant his patron; somewhat of which appears in the tale of *Piers Plowman*: [21] yet I cannot blame him for inveighing so sharply against the vices of the clergy in his age: their pride, their ambition, their pomp, their avarice, their worldly interest, deserved the lashes which he gave them, both in that, and in most of his *Canterbury Tales*. Neither has his contemporary Boccace spared them: yet both those poets lived in much esteem with good and holy men in orders; for the scandal which is given by particular priests reflects not on the sacred function. Chaucer's Monk, his Canon, and his Friar, took not from the character of his Good Parson. A satirical poet is the check of the laymen on bad priests. We are only to take care, that we involve not the innocent with the guilty in the same

[21] Dryden is here referring to "The Plowman's Tale," a work of unknown authorship that was thought at the time to be by Chaucer. This tale is not to be confused with *Piers Plowman*, a long fourteenth-century poem by William Langland.

condemnation. The good cannot be too much honoured, nor the bad too coarsely used; for the corruption of the best becomes the worst. When a clergyman is whipped, his gown is first taken off, by which the dignity of his order is secured. If he be wrongfully accused, he has his action of slander; and 'tis at the poet's peril if he transgress the law. But they will tell us, that all kind of satire, though never so well deserved by particular priests, yet brings the whole order into contempt. Is then the peerage of England anything dishonoured when a peer suffers for his treason? If he be libelled, or any way defamed, he has his *scandalum magnatum* [22] to punish the offender. They who use this kind of argument, seems to be conscious to themselves of somewhat which has deserved the poet's lash, and are less concerned for their public capacity than for their private; at least there is pride at the bottom of their reasoning. If the faults of men in orders are only to be judged among themselves, they are all in some sort parties; for, since they say the honour of their order is concerned in every member of it, how can we be sure that they will be impartial judges? How far I may be allowed to speak my opinion in this case, I know not; but I am sure a dispute of this nature caused mischief in abundance betwixt a King of England and an Archbishop of Canterbury; one standing up for the laws of his land, and the other for the honour (as he called it) of God's Church; which ended in the murder of the prelate, and in the whipping of his Majesty from post to pillar for his penance.[23] The learned and ingenious Dr. Drake [24] has saved me the labour of inquiring into the esteem and reverence which the priests have had of old; and I would rather extend than diminish any part of it: yet I must needs say, that when a priest provokes me without any occasion given

22 "Law of extraordinary slander."

23 Dryden is referring to the murder of Thomas à Becket at the order of Henry II in 1170.

24 James Drake (1667–1707) wrote a retort to Jeremy Collier in *The Ancient and Modern Stage Reviewed, or Mr. Collier's View of the Immorality and Profaneness of the Stage Set in a True Light* (1699).

him, I have no reason, unless it be the charity of a Christian, to forgive him: *prior laesit* [25] is justification sufficient in the civil law. If I answer him in his own language, self-defence, I am sure must be allowed me; and if I carry it further, even to a sharp recrimination, somewhat may be indulged to human frailty. Yet my resentment has not wrought so far, but that I have followed Chaucer, in his character of a holy man, and have enlarged on that subject with some pleasure; reserving to myself the right, if I shall think fit hereafter, to describe another sort of priests, such as are more easily to be found than the Good Parson; such as have given the last blow to Christianity in this age, by a practice so contrary to their doctrine. But this will keep cold till another time. In the meanwhile, I take up Chaucer where I left him.

He must have been a man of a most wonderful comprehensive nature, because, as it has been truly observed of him, he has taken into the compass of his *Canterbury Tales* the various manners and humours (as we now call them) of the whole English nation, in his age. Not a single character has escaped him. All his pilgrims are severally distinguished from each other; and not only in their inclinations, but in their very physiognomies and persons. Baptista Porta [26] could not have described their natures better, than by the marks which the poet gives them. The matter and manner of their tales, and of their telling, are so suited to their different educations, humours, and callings, that each of them would be improper in any other mouth. Even the grave and serious characters are distinguished by their several sorts of gravity: their discourses are such as belong to their age, their calling, and their breeding; such as are becoming of them, and of them only. Some of his persons are vicious, and some virtuous; some are unlearn'd, or (as Chaucer calls them) lewd, and some are learn'd. Even the ribaldry of the low characters is different: the Reeve, the Miller, and the Cook, are several men, and distinguished from

[25] "He committed the first offense" (Terence, *Eunuch* 6).

[26] Giambattista della Porta (1538–1615), Italian physicist and physiognomist.

each other as much as the mincing Lady-Prioress and the broad-speaking, gap-toothed Wife of Bath. But enough of this; there is such a variety of game springing up before me, that I am distracted in my choice, and know not which to follow. 'Tis sufficient to say according to the proverb, that here is God's plenty. We have our forefathers and great-grand-dames all before us, as they were in Chaucer's days; their general characters are still remaining in mankind, and even in England, though they are called by other names than those of Monks, and Friars, and Canons, and Lady Abbesses, and Nuns; for mankind is ever the same, and nothing lost out of Nature, though everything is altered. May I have leave to do myself the justice (since my enemies will do me none, and are so far from granting me to be a good poet, that they will not allow me so much as to be a Christian, or a moral man), may I have leave, I say, to inform my reader, that I have confined my choice to such tales of Chaucer as savour nothing of immodesty. If I had desired more to please then to instruct, the Reeve, the Miller, the Shipman, the Merchant, the Sumner, and, above all, the Wife of Bath, in the *Prologue* to her *Tale,* would have procured me as many friends and readers, as there are *beaux* and ladies of pleasure in the town. But I will no more offend against good manners: I am sensible as I ought to be of the scandal I have given by my loose writings; and make what reparation I am able, by this public acknowledgment. If anything of this nature, or of profaneness, be crept into these poems, I am so far from defending it, that I disown it. *Totum hoc indictum volo.*[27] Chaucer makes another manner of apology for his broad speaking, and Boccace makes the like; but I will follow neither of them. Our countryman, in the end of his Characters, before the *Canterbury Tales,* thus excuses the ribaldry, which is very gross, in many of his novels:

> *But firste, I pray you, of your courtesy,*
> *That ye ne arrete it nought my villany,*
> *Though that I plainly speak in this mattere*

27 "I wish all of it unsaid" (source unidentified).

> *To tellen you her words, and eke her chere:*
> *Ne though I speak her words properly,*
> *For this ye knowen as well as I,*
> *Who shall tellen a tale after a man*
> *He mote rehearse as nye, as ever He can:*
> *Everich word of it ben in his charge,*
> All speke he, never so rudely, ne large:
> *Or else he mote tellen his tale untrue,*
> *Or feine things, or find words new:*
> *He may not spare, altho he were his brother,*
> *He mote as wel say o word as another.*
> Crist *spake himself ful broad in holy Writ,*
> *And well I wote no Villany is it.*
> Eke *Plato saith, who so can him rede,*
> *The words mote been Cousin to the dede.*[28]

Yet if a man should have enquired of Boccace or of
Chaucer, what need they had of introducing such characters,
where obscene words were proper in their mouths, but very
undecent to be heard; I know not what answer they could
have made; for that reason, such tales shall be left untold
by me. You have here a *Specimen* of Chaucer's language,
which is so obsolete, that his sense is scarce to be understood;
and you have likewise more than one example of his unequal
numbers, which were mentioned before. Yet many of his verses
consist of ten syllables, and the words not much behind our
present English: as for example, these two lines, in the description of the Carpenter's young wife:

> *Wincing she was, as is a jolly Colt,*
> *Long as a Mast, and upright as a Bolt.*[29]

I have almost done with Chaucer, when I have answered
some objections relating to my present work. I find some people are offended that I have turned these tales into modern
English; because they think them unworthy of my pains, and
look on Chaucer as a dry, old-fashioned wit, not worth re-
viving. I have often heard the late Earl of Leicester say, that
Mr. Cowley himself was of that opinion; who, having read

---

28 *Canterbury Tales*, "General Prologue," A. 725–742.
29 *Ibid.*, "Miller's Tale," A. 3263–3264.

him over at my Lord's request, declared he had no taste of him. I dare not advance my opinion against the judgment of so great an author; but I think it fair, however, to leave the decision to the public. Mr. Cowley was too modest to set up for a dictator; and being shocked perhaps with his old style, never examined into the depth of his good sense. Chaucer, I confess, is a rough diamond, and must first be polished ere he shines. I deny not likewise, that, living in our early days of poetry, he writes not always of a piece; but sometimes mingles trivial things with those of greater moment. Sometimes also, though not often, he runs riot, like Ovid, and knows not when he has said enough. But there are more great wits besides Chaucer, whose fault is their excess of conceits, and those ill sorted. An author is not to write all he can, but only all he ought. Having observed this redundancy in Chaucer (as it is an easy matter for a man of ordinary parts to find a fault in one of greater), I have not tied myself to a literal translation; but have often omitted what I judged unnecessary, or not of dignity enough to appear in the company of better thoughts. I have presumed farther in some places, and added somewhat of my own where I thought my author was deficient, and had not given his thoughts their true lustre, for want of words in the beginning of our language. And to this I was the more emboldened, because (if I may be permitted to say it of myself) I found I had a soul congenial to his, and that I had been conversant in the same studies. Another poet, in another age, may take the same liberty with my writings; if at least they live long enough to deserve correction. It was also necessary sometimes to restore the sense of Chaucer, which was lost or mangled in the errors of the press. Let this example suffice at present: in the story of *Palamon and Arcite*, where the temple of Diana is described, you find these verses, in all the editions of our author:

> There saw I Danè *turned unto a Tree,*
> *I mean not the Goddess* Diane,
> *But* Venus *Daughter, which that hight* Danè.[30]

[30] *Ibid.*, "Knight's Tale," A. 2062–2064.

Which after a little consideration I knew was to be reformed into this sense, that Daphne the daughter of Peneus was turned into a tree. I durst not make thus bold with Ovid, lest some future Milbourne [31] should arise and say, I varied from my author, because I understood him not.

But there are other judges, who think I ought not to have translated Chaucer into English, out of a quite contrary notion: they suppose there is a certain veneration due to his old language; and that it is little less than profanation and sacrilege to alter it. They are farther of opinion, that somewhat of his good sense will suffer in this transfusion, and much of the beauty of his thoughts will infallibly be lost, which appear with more grace in their old habit. Of this opinion was that excellent person whom I mentioned, the late Earl of Leicester, who valued Chaucer as much as Mr. Cowley despised him. My Lord dissuaded me from this attempt (for I was thinking of it some years before his death), and his authority prevailed so far with me, as to defer my undertaking it while he lived, in deference to him: yet my reason was not convinced with what he urged against it. If the first end of a writer be to be understood, then, as his language grows obsolete, his thoughts must grow obscure—

> *Multa renascentur, quae nunc cecidere; cadentque*
> *Quae nunc sunt in honore vocabula, si volet usus,*
> *Quem penes arbitrium est et jus et norma loquendi.*[32]

When an ancient word for its sound and significancy deserves to be revived, I have that reasonable veneration for antiquity to restore it. All beyond this is superstition. Words are not like landmarks, so sacred as never to be removed; customs are changed, and even statutes are silently repealed, when the reason ceases for which they were enacted. As for the other part of the argument, that his thoughts will lose of their original beauty by the innovation of words; in the first

---

[31] Luke Milbourne (1649–1720), a clergyman who had criticized Dryden's Virgil.

[32] See above, p. 23, footnote 29.

place, not only their beauty, but their being is lost, where they are no longer understood, which is the present case. I grant that something must be lost in all transfusion, that is, in all translations; but the sense will remain, which would otherwise be lost, or at least be maimed, when it is scarce intelligible, and that but to a few. How few are there who can read Chaucer, so as to understand him perfectly? And if imperfectly, then with less profit, and no pleasure. 'Tis not for the use of some old Saxon friends, that I have taken these pains with him: let them neglect my version, because they have no need of it. I made it for their sakes who understand sense and poetry as well as they, when that poetry and sense is put into words which they understand. I will go farther, and dare to add, that what beauties I lose in some places, I give to others which had them not originally: but in this I may be partial to myself; let the reader judge, and I submit to his decision. Yet I think I have just occasion to complain of them, who because they understand Chaucer, would deprive the greater part of their countrymen of the same advantage, and hoard him up, as misers do their grandam gold, only to look on it themselves, and hinder others from making use of it. In sum, I seriously protest, that no man ever had, or can have, a greater veneration for Chaucer than myself. I have translated some part of his works, only that I might perpetuate his memory, or at least refresh it, amongst my countrymen. If I have altered him anywhere for the better, I must at the same time acknowledge, that I could have done nothing without him. *Facile est inventis addere* [33] is no great commendation; and I am not so vain to think I have deserved a greater. I will conclude what I have to say of him singly, with this one remark: A lady of my acquaintance, who keeps a kind of correspondence with some authors of the fair sex in France, has been informed by them, that Mademoiselle de Scudery, who is as old as Sibyl, and inspired like her by the same God of Poetry, is at this time translating Chaucer into modern French.

[33] "It is easy to add to what has already been discovered" (source unidentified).

From which I gather, that he has been formerly translated into the old Provençal; for how she should come to understand old English, I know not. But the matter of fact being true, it makes me think that there is something in it like fatality; that, after certain periods of time, the fame and memory of great Wits should be renewed, as Chaucer is both in France and England. If this be wholly chance, 'tis extraordinary; and I dare not call it more, for fear of being taxed with superstition.

Boccace comes last to be considered, who, living in the same age with Chaucer, had the same genius, and followed the same studies. Both writ novels, and each of them cultivated his mother tongue. But the greatest resemblance of our two modern authors being in their familiar style, and pleasing way of relating comical adventures, I may pass it over, because I have translated nothing from Boccace of that nature. In the serious part of poetry, the advantage is wholly on Chaucer's side; for though the Englishman has borrowed many tales from the Italian, yet it appears, that those of Boccace were not generally of his own making, but taken from authors of former ages, and by him only modelled; so that what there was of invention, in either of them, may be judged equal. But Chaucer has refined on Boccace, and has mended the stories, which he has borrowed, in his way of telling; though prose allows more liberty of thought, and the expression is more easy when unconfined by numbers. Our countryman carries weight, and yet wins the race at disadvantage. I desire not the reader should take my word; and, therefore, I will set two of their discourses, on the same subject, in the same light, for every man to judge betwixt them. I translated Chaucer first, and, amongst the rest, pitched on the Wife of Bath's Tale; not daring, as I have said, to adventure on her *Prologue,* because 'tis too licentious. There Chaucer introduces an old woman, of mean parentage, whom a youthful knight, of noble blood, was forced to marry, and consequently loathed her. The crone being in bed with him on the wedding-night, and finding his aversion, endeavours to win his affection by reason, and speaks a good word for herself (as who could blame her?) in hope to mollify the sullen bridegroom. She takes her topics from the benefits of poverty, the advantages of old age and ugliness, the vanity of youth, and the silly pride of ancestry and titles, without inherent virtue, which is the true nobility. When I had closed Chaucer, I returned to Ovid, and translated some more of his fables; and, by this time, had so far forgotten the Wife of Bath's Tale, that, when I took up Boccace, unawares I fell on the same argument, of preferring virtue to nobility of blood and titles, in the story of *Sigismonda;* which I had certainly avoided, for the resemblance of the two discourses, if my memory had not failed me. Let the reader weigh them both; and, if he thinks me partial to Chaucer, 'tis in him to right Boccace.

I prefer, in our countryman, far above all his other stories, the noble poem of Palamon and Arcite, which is of the epic kind, and perhaps not much inferior to the *Ilias,* or the *Aeneis.* The story is more pleasing than either of them, the manners as perfect, the diction as poetical, the learning as deep and various, and the disposition full as artful: only it includes a greater length of time, as taking up seven years at least; but Aristotle has left undecided the duration of the action; which yet is easily reduced into the compass of a year, by a narration of what preceded the return of Palamon to Athens. I had thought, for the honour of our narration, and more particularly for his, whose laurel, though unworthy, I have worn after him, that this story was of English growth, and Chaucer's own: but I was undeceived by Boccace; for, casually looking on the end of his seventh *Giornata,* I found Dioneo (under which name he shadows himself) and Fiametta (who represents his mistress, the natural daughter of Robert, King of Naples), of whom these words are spoken: *Dioneo e Fiametta gran pezza cantarono insieme d'Arcita, e di Palemone,*[34] by which it appears, that this story was written before the time of Boccace; but the name of its author being wholly lost, Chaucer

[34] "Dione and Fiametta sang together for a long time of Arcite and Palamon" (*Decameron,* VII, 10, the epilogue).

is now become an original; and I question not but the poem has received many beauties, by passing through his noble hands. Besides this tale, there is another of his own invention, after the manner of the Provençals, called *The Flower and the Leaf*,[35] with which I was so particularly pleased, both for the invention and the moral, that I cannot hinder myself from recommending it to the reader.

As a corollary to this preface, in which I have done justice to others, I owe somewhat to myself: not that I think it worth my time to enter the lists with one M——, or one B——,[36] but barely to take notice, that such men there are, who have written scurrilously against me, without any provocation. M——, who is in orders, pretends, amongst the rest, this quarrel to me, that I have fallen foul on priesthood: if I have, I am only to ask pardon of good priests, and am afraid his part of the reparation will come to little. Let him be satisfied, that he shall not be able to force himself upon me for an adversary. I contemn him too much to enter into competition with him. His own translations of Virgil have answered his criticisms on mine. If (as they say, he has declared in print) he prefers the version of Ogilby [37] to mine, the world has made him the same compliment; for 'tis agreed on all hands, that he writes even below Ogilby. That, you will say, is not easily to be done; but what cannot M—— bring about? I am satisfied, however, that, while he and I live together, I shall not be thought the worst poet of the age. It looks as if I had desired him underhand to write so ill against me; but upon my honest word I have not bribed him to do me this service, and am wholly guiltless of his pamphlet. 'Tis true, I should be glad if I could persuade him to continue his good offices, and write such another critique on anything of mine; for I find, by experience, he has a great stroke with the reader, when he con-

35 *The Flower and the Leaf* is a fifteenth-century poem of uncertain authorship but in Dryden's time was regarded as Chaucer's work.

36 Milbourne and Sir Richard Blackmore (*ca.* 1653–1729), the English poet.

37 John Ogilby (1600–1676), translator of Homer and Virgil.

demns any of my poems, to make the world have a better opinion of them. He has taken some pains with my poetry; but
nobody will be persuaded to take the same with his. If I had
taken to the Church (as he affirms, but which was never in my
thoughts) I should have had more sense, if not more grace,
than to have turned myself out of my benefice, by writing
libels on my parishioners. But his account of my manners and
my principles are of a piece with his cavils and his poetry;
and so I have done with him for ever.

As for the City Bard, or Knight Physician,[38] I hear his quarrel to me is, that I was the author of *Absalom and Achitophel,*
which, he thinks, is a little hard on his fanatic patrons in
London.

But I will deal the more civilly with his two poems, because
nothing ill is to be spoken of the dead; and therefore peace
be to the *Manes* of his *Arthurs.*[39] I will only say, that it was
not for this noble Knight that I drew the plan of an epic
poem on *King Arthur,* in my preface to the translation of
Juvenal. The Guardian Angels of kingdoms were machines
too ponderous for him to manage; and therefore he rejected
them as Dares did the whirl-bats of Eryx when they were
thrown before him by Entellus:[40] yet from that preface he
plainly took his hint; for he began immediately upon the
story, though he had the baseness not to acknowledge his
benefactor, but instead of it, to traduce me in a libel.

I shall say the less of Mr. Collier,[41] because in many things
he has taxed me justly; and I have pleaded guilty to all
thoughts and expressions of mine, which can be truly argued
of obscenity, profaneness, or immorality, and retract them. If
he be my enemy, let him triumph; if he be my friend, as I
have given him no personal occasion to be otherwise, he will
be glad of my repentance. It becomes me not to draw my pen

---

[38] Blackmore.
[39] *Prince Arthur* and *King Arthur,* Blackmore's epics.
[40] Cf. Virgil, *Aeneid* V. 400–403.
[41] See above, p. 98, footnote 8.

in the defence of a bad cause, when I have so often drawn it
for a good one. Yet it were not difficult to prove, that in many
places he has perverted my meaning by his glosses, and inter-
preted my words into blasphemy and bawdry, of which they
were not guilty. Besides that, he is too much given to horse-
play in his raillery, and comes to battle like a dictator from
the plough. I will not say, *The Zeal of God's House has eaten
him up;* [42] but I am sure it has devoured some part of his
good manners and civility. It might also be doubted, whether
it were altogether zeal which prompted him to this rough
manner of proceeding; perhaps it became not one of his function to rake into the rubbish of ancient and modern plays; a
divine might have employed his pains to better purpose, than
in the nastiness of Plautus and Aristophanes, whose examples,
as they excuse not me, so it might be possibly supposed, that
he read them not without some pleasure. They who have
written commentaries on those poets, or on Horace, Juvenal,
and Martial, have explained some vices, which without their
interpretation had been unknown to modern times. Neither
has he judged impartially betwixt the former age and us.
There is more bawdry in one play of Fletcher's, called *The
Custom of the Country,* than in all ours together. Yet this has
been often acted on the stage in my remembrance. Are the
times so much more reformed now, than they were five-and-
twenty years ago? If they are, I congratulate the amendment of
our morals. But I am not to prejudice the cause of my fellow-
poets, though I abandon my own defence: they have some of
them answered for themselves, and neither they nor I can
think Mr. Collier so formidable an enemy that we should
shun him. He has lost ground at the latter end of the day,
by pursuing his point too far, like the Prince of Condé at the
battle of Senneph: [43] from immoral plays to no plays, *ab abusu
ad usum, non valet consequentia.* [44] But being a party, I am

42 Psalms 69:9; John 2:17.

43 Fought on August 11, 1674.

44 "To apply the abuse of something to its use is not a valid way of
reasoning" (a traditional rule used by logicians).

not to erect myself into a judge. As for the rest of those who
have written against me, they are such scoundrels, that they
deserve not the least notice to be taken of them. B—— and
M—— are only distinguished from the crowd by being re-
membered to their infamy:

> . . . *Demetri, teque Tigelli,*
> *Discipulorum inter jubeo plorare cathedras.*[45]

[45] "I command you, Demetrius and Tigelus, to lament amidst the
seats of your scholars" (Horace, *Satires* I. 10. 90–91).

The Library of Liberal Arts

Below is a representative selection from The Library of Liberal Arts. This partial listing—taken from the more than 200 scholarly editions of the world's finest literature and philosophy—indicates the scope, nature, and concept of this distinguished series.